The Happiest Man on Earth

Eddie Jaku OAM was born Abraham Jakubowicz in Germany in 1920. In World War II, Eddie was imprisoned in Buchenwald and Auschwitz concentration camps. In 1945, he was sent on a death march but escaped. Finally, he was rescued by Allied soldiers.

In 1950, he moved with family to Australia. Eddie volunteered at the Sydney Jewish Museum since its inception in 1992.

Eddie and Flore were married for seventy-five years, with two sons, and many grandchildren and great-grandchildren.

He died in October 2021, at the age of 101. His book has been translated into thirty-seven languages and his message continues to be shared around the world.

The Happiest Man on Earth

EDDIE JAKU

PAN BOOKS

First published 2020 by Pan Macmillan Australia Pty Ltd

First published in the UK 2020 by Macmillan

This paperback edition first published 2022 by Pan Books
an imprint of Pan Macmillan
The Smithson, 6 Briset Street, London EC1M 5NR
EU representative: Macmillan Publishers Ireland Ltd, 1st Floor,
The Liffey Trust Centre, 117–126 Sheriff Street Upper,
Dublin 1, D01 YC43
Associated companies throughout the world
www.panmacmillan.com

ISBN 978-1-5290-6636-4

135798642

A CIP catalogue record for this book is available from the British Library.

Aboriginal and Torres Strait Islander people should be aware that this
book may contain images or names of people now deceased.

Printed and bound by CPI Group (UK) Ltd, Croydon, CR0 4YY

MIX
Paper from
responsible sources
FSC® C116313

Visit **www.panmacmillan.com** to read more about all our books
and to buy them. You will also find features, author interviews and
news of any author events, and you can sign up for e-newsletters
so that you're always first to hear about our new releases.

For future generations

Don't walk behind me, I may not lead.

Don't walk in front of me, I may not follow.

Just walk beside me and be my friend.

– Anonymous

PROLOGUE

MY DEAR NEW FRIEND.

I have lived for a century, and I know what it is to stare evil in the face. I have seen the very worst in mankind, the horrors of the death camps, the Nazi efforts to exterminate my life, and the lives of all my people.

But I now consider myself the happiest man on Earth.

Through all of my years I have learned this: life can be beautiful if you make it beautiful.

I will tell you my story. It is a sad one in parts, with great darkness and great sorrow. But it is a happy story in the end because happiness is something we can choose. It is up to you.

I will show you how.

CHAPTER ONE

*There are many things more
precious than money.*

I WAS BORN IN 1920 IN A CITY CALLED LEIPZIG, IN eastern Germany. My name was Abraham Salomon Jakubowicz, but friends called me Adi for short. In English, the name is pronounced Eddie. So please, call me Eddie, my friend.

We were a loving family, a big family. My father, Isidore, had four brothers and three sisters, and my mum, Lina, was one of thirteen children. Imagine the strength of my grandmother, who raised so many children! She lost a son in the First World War, a Jew who sacrificed his life for Germany, as well as her husband, my grandfather, an army chaplain who never returned from the war.

My father was as proud a German citizen as could be, an immigrant from Poland who settled in Germany. He first left Poland as an apprentice in fine mechanical engineering for typewriter manufacturer Remington.

Because he spoke good German, he made his way to America working on a German merchant ship.

He excelled in his trade in America, but missed his family and decided to travel back to Europe to visit on another German merchant ship – arriving just in time to be caught in the First World War. Because he was travelling on a Polish passport, he was interned by the Germans as an illegal alien. However, the German government recognised that he was a skilled mechanic, and allowed him to leave internment to work in a factory in Leipzig, making heavy weapons for the war effort. In this time he fell in love with my mother, Lina, and with Germany, and stayed after the war. He opened a factory in Leipzig, married my mother, and soon I was born. Two years later, we welcomed my little sister Johanna into the world. We called her Henni for short.

Nothing could shake my father's patriotism and pride in Germany. We considered ourselves Germans first, Germans second, and then Jewish. Our religion did not seem as important to us as being good citizens of our Leipzig. We practised our traditions and observed our holidays, but our loyalty and our love were for Germany. I was proud to come from Leipzig, which had for 800 years been a centre for art and culture – it had one of the oldest symphony orchestras in the world, and it was a city that inspired Johann Sebastian Bach, Clara Schumann, Felix

Mendelssohn, writers, poets and philosophers – Goethe, Liebniz and Nietzsche, and many others.

For centuries, Jews had been part of the very fabric of Leipzig society. Since medieval times, the big market day was on Friday, rather than Saturday, to allow Jewish merchants to participate, as work is forbidden for us on Saturday, the Jewish Sabbath. Prominent Jewish citizens and philanthropists contributed to the public good, as well as the Jewish community, overseeing the construction of some of Europe's most beautiful synagogues. Harmony was part of life. And it was a very good life for a child. We had the zoological gardens just five minutes' walk from my house, famed around the world for its collection and for breeding more lions in captivity than anywhere else in the world. Can you imagine how exciting it was for a small boy? We had huge trade fairs twice a year that my father would take me to – the same ones that had made Leipzig one of the most cultured and wealthy cities in Europe. Leipzig's location and importance as a trading city made it a nexus for the spread of new technologies and ideas. Its university, Germany's second oldest, was founded in 1409. The world's first daily newspaper began publication in Leipzig in 1650. A city of books, of music, of opera. As a boy, I truly believed that I was part of the most enlightened, most cultured, most sophisticated – certainly the most educated – society in the whole world. How wrong I was.

While I was not personally very religious, we visited synagogue regularly. We kept a kosher kitchen and diet for my mother, who wanted to do things as traditionally as possible to please her mother, my grandmother who lived with us and who was very religious. Each Friday night we would meet for *Shabbos* (Sabbath) dinner, say our prayers, and eat traditional meals lovingly prepared by my grandmother. She would cook on the huge wood stove that also heated the house. An ingenious system of pipes ran through the home so that spare heat was not wasted, and the smoke was taken safely outside. When we came in frozen from the outside, we would sit on cushions next to that stove to warm up. I had a dog, a little dachshund puppy called Lulu, who would curl up on my lap on cold nights. How I treasured those nights.

My father worked hard to provide for us and we were comfortable, but he was careful to make sure we understood that there was much more to life than material things. Each Friday night, before the *Shabbos* dinner, Mother would bake three or four loaves of *challah*, the special, richly delicious ceremonial bread made with eggs and flour that we ate on special occasions. When I was six, I asked him why we baked so many when we were only a family of four, and he explained that he would take the extra loaves to the synagogue to give to Jews in need. He loved his family, and his friends. He was always bringing friends home to share dinner with us, although my mother put her foot down and said he could have no more than five people at a time, as no more could squeeze around our table.

'If you are lucky enough to have money and a nice house, you can afford to help those who don't,' he would tell me. 'This is what life is all about. To share your good fortune.' My father used to say to me there is more pleasure in giving than in taking, that the important things in life – friends, family, kindness – are far more precious than money. A man is worth more than his bank account. I thought he was crazy then, but now after all I have seen in this life, I know he was right.

But there was a cloud over our happy family scene. Germany was in trouble. We had lost the last war and the economy was ruined. The victorious Allied powers demanded more money in reparations than Germany could ever pay back, and 68 million people were suffering. There were food and fuel shortages and rampant poverty, which was keenly felt by the very proud German people. Although we were a comfortable middle-class family, it was not possible to find many necessities, even with ready money. My mother would walk many kilometres to market to exchange handbags and clothes she'd collected in better times for eggs, milk, butter or bread. For my thirteenth birthday, my father asked me what I wanted, and I asked for six eggs, a loaf of white bread, which was hard to find as Germans prefer rye bread, and a pineapple. I couldn't imagine anything more impressive than six eggs, and I had never seen a pineapple. And somehow, he found one – I have no idea how, but that was my father. He would do things that seemed impossible just to put a smile on my face. I was so excited that I ate all six eggs and the whole pineapple at once. I'd never had so much rich food. Mum warned me to slow down but did I listen? No!

Inflation was terrible, which made it impossible to stock up on non-perishable foods or to plan for the future. My father would come home from work with a valise full of cash that would be worthless by morning. He would send me to the store and say, 'Buy whatever you can! If there are six loaves of bread, get them all! Tomorrow we will have nothing!' It was very hard even for fortunate people to live, and the Germans were humiliated and angry. People became desperate and receptive to any solution. The Nazi party and Hitler promised the German people a solution. And they provided an enemy.

In 1933, when Hitler came to power, he brought with him a wave of anti-Semitism. This was my thirteenth year, and our tradition called for my *Bar Mitzvah*, an ancient religious ceremony to celebrate coming-of-age. *Bar Mitzvah*, meaning 'son of commandment', is usually followed by a wonderful party with delicious food and dancing. In other times, it would have been held in the grand Leipzig Synagogue, but this wasn't permitted after Nazi rule began. Instead, I had my *Bar Mitzvah* in a small synagogue three hundred metres down the street. The Rabbi who ran our *shul* (another name for synagogue, literally 'house of books') was very smart. He rented the flat below the synagogue to a gentile who had a son in the SS. When anti-Semitic attacks came, this gentile son always made sure guards were protecting the flat, and therefore the *shul* above it. If they wanted to destroy the *shul*, they would have to destroy this man's home too.

We had the religious ceremony, with candle lighting and prayers for both my family, and those who had passed away. After the ceremony, I was considered a man in Jewish tradition, responsible for my own actions. I started to think about my future.

As a very small boy, I had wanted to be a doctor, but that was not where my talents lay. In Germany, we had centres to which students were sent to discover their aptitudes through a series of memory and manual dexterity tests. From that they decided that my talents were optical and mathematical, with excellent eyesight and hand-eye co-ordination. I would make a fine engineer, so this was what I decided to study.

I was attending a very good school in a beautiful building called 32 Volkschule. It was one kilometre away from our home, and it would take me about fifteen minutes to walk there. Unless it was winter! Leipzig is a very cold city and for eight months of the year, the river was frozen solid. I could skate on the river all the way to school in five minutes.

In 1933, I graduated to high school, and would attend the Leibniz Gymnasium school. Had history run a different course, I would have studied there until I was 18, but it was not to be.

One day, I turned up and was informed I could no longer attend – I was being kicked out for being Jewish. This was unacceptable to my father, a stubborn man with powerful connections in Leipzig, who soon devised a new plan for my education.

'Don't worry,' he said to me. 'You will continue your studies. I will make sure.'

False papers were prepared for me, and with the help of a family friend I was enrolled at Jeter und Shearer, a mechanical engineering college in Tuttlingen, far to the south of Leipzig. This was the epicentre of engineering technology in the world at that time, supplying the world with precision mechanics. They made all kinds of incredible machines, intricate medical instruments and industrial machinery. I remember seeing a machine where a chicken would go into one end of a conveyer belt and emerge at the other end plucked, washed, and wrapped. It was incredible! And I would be learning how to make these machines, the best possible engineering education in the world. To get in, I had to sit a series of exams, and I was so nervous that I had to be careful to wipe the sweat from my forehead before it could fall and ruin my paper. I was very anxious that I would let my father down.

I was enrolled under the assumed name of Walter Schleif, a gentile German orphan who had less to fear from Hitler's appointment as German chancellor. Walter Schleif was the identity of a real German boy who had vanished. Most likely, his family had quietly left Germany when the Nazis began to rise. My father obtained his identity cards and was able to modify them into forgeries that were convincing enough to fool the government. German identity cards at the time had tiny photos embedded in the paper which could only be seen with a special infrared light. The forgery had to be very well done, but my father's vocation in typewriters meant he had access to the right tools and know-how.

With the new documents, I could begin a new life and take my place in the school, where I began an apprenticeship in mechanical engineering. The school was a nine-hour train journey from Leipzig. I would have to look after myself, my clothes, my education, and keep my secret at all costs. I would attend school every day and sleep at night in a nearby orphanage, in a dormitory with much older boys. In return for the work of my appren-ticeship, I received a small stipend which I could use for clothing and other essentials.

It was a lonely existence, being Walter Schleif. I could tell nobody who I really was, could confide in nobody – to do so would have meant the outing of my Jewish identity and put me in danger. I had to take special care in the restrooms and shower, as if another boy were to notice I was circumcised, it would have been the end for me.

There was little contact with home. Writing letters was not safe, and to telephone I had to visit the phone in a department store basement, taking a long and compli-cated route to make sure I wasn't followed. On the rare occasions I could speak to my family, it broke my heart. I can't begin to explain the pain of being a young man so far from home, and that being the only possibility to secure an education and the future my father wanted for me. But as hard as it was to be far from my family, it would have been worse to let them down.

I told my father how lonely I was without them, and he urged me to be strong.

'Eddie, I know it is very difficult, but one day you will thank me,' he would say. I learned later that although he was stern with me, the moment after he hung up the phone, he would start crying like a baby. He was putting on a brave face to help make me brave.

And he was right. Without what I learned at that school, I would never have survived what was to come.

Five years passed. Five years of unrelenting work and loneliness.

I'm not sure I can explain what it is like to pretend to be someone you are not from thirteen-and-a-half to eighteen. It is a terrible burden to carry that secret for so long. Not a moment passed when I did not miss my family, but I understood that my studies were important and persisted. It was a terrible sacrifice, to miss my family for so long, but I gained so much from my education.

In the final years of my apprenticeship, I worked at a company making very fine X-ray equipment. In addition to the technical and theoretical side of my education, I was expected to demonstrate that I could work hard and capably at my new profession. I would work all day and attend school at night. Wednesday was the only day I didn't work and could devote entirely to my studies.

Despite my loneliness, I loved the education I was getting. The masters I was studying under were some of the greatest minds in the world, and they could pick up their tools and make seemingly anything, from the tiniest gears to giant machines on the forefront of technology.

It all seemed miraculous to me. Germany was at the fore-front of a technological and industrial revolution that promised to make quality of life better for millions of people, and I was on the very cutting edge.

In 1938, just after my eighteenth birthday, I sat my final exams, and was selected as the top apprentice of the year from my school and invited to join the union. The unions in Germany at that time were not the same as you find in modern society. They had less to do with negotiating work conditions and how much money you made, and were more about what you were able to do as a practitioner. At that time, you were only invited to join if you were really good at your profession, the top of your trade. It was a place for the finest minds in a field to gather and co-operate to push science and industry forward. Within the union, concerns like class and creed had no importance next to the prestige of the work itself. It was truly a great honour for me to be admitted so young.

At the ceremony, I was called up in front of everyone to accept the commendation from the Master of the Precision Engineering Union, who was dressed in the traditional fine blue robe with an elaborate lace collar.

'Today, we accept the apprentice Walter Schleif into one of the finest unions in Germany,' announced the Master. I burst into tears.

The Master shook me. 'What's wrong with you? This is one of your finest days! You should be proud!'

But I was inconsolable. I felt terribly sad that my parents couldn't be there to see me. I wanted so badly for them to see what I had achieved – wanted, too, for my master to understand that I wasn't the poor orphan, Walter Schleif. That I was Eddie Jaku, that I had a family who loved me, and it hurt so much to be far from them.

I treasure every piece of knowledge those years gave me, but I will always regret that time spent far from my family. Truly, my father was wise when he told me a life is worth more than a bank account. There are many things in this world that no amount of money will buy you, and some things priceless beyond measure. Family first, family second, and family at the last.

CHAPTER TWO

Weakness can be turned into hatred.

I MADE THE BIGGEST MISTAKE OF MY YOUNG LIFE ON 9 November 1938.

After I graduated, I took a job making precision medical instruments and remained in Tuttlingen for several months. It was my parents' 20th wedding anniversary and I resolved to surprise them with a visit. I bought myself a ticket and made the nine-hour train trip to the city where I was born. Outside the window, the fields and forests of Germany rolled by.

In the sheltered confines of the school, I'd had no access to newspapers or radio. I had no idea what had been happening to the country I loved so much, or about the growing cloud of anti-Semitism that had settled over the land.

I arrived home and found the house dark and locked up. My family had vanished. I wasn't to know that they had gone into hiding, believing that I was safe and far away.

I still had my key, otherwise I would have had to sleep in the gutter. I opened my door, and there was my dachshund, Lulu. She immediately jumped up and licked my legs. She was happy, and so was I.

I was very worried about my family. It did not make sense to me that they would be gone in the middle of the night. But I was very tired and in my childhood bed after five years away. It did not seem possible that anything bad could happen to me there.

I lay awake, listening to far off noises in the street. I had no idea what was happening, that across the city, synagogues were burning. Eventually, exhausted, I fell asleep.

I awoke at 5 am to the sound of the door being kicked. Ten Nazis broke in, dragged me from bed and, I swear to you, they beat me half to death. My pyjamas were soon soaked with my blood. One took his bayonet, cut off my sleeve, and started to engrave a swastika in my arm. As he started cutting, my little dog Lulu jumped on him. I don't know if she bit him or just scared him, but the Nazi let me go and then, using the bayonet at the end of his rifle, stabbed and killed my poor little dog, shouting, '*Ein Juden Hund*!' Jewish Dog.

I thought, Eddie, this is your last day. Today, you're going to die.

But they were not there to kill me, only to beat and

humiliate me. After their first attack, they dragged me into the street and made me witness the destruction of our 200-year-old house, the home generations of my family had been raised in. In that moment, I lost my dignity, my freedom and my faith in humanity. I lost everything I lived for. I was reduced from a man to being nothing.

That night is now infamous as *Kristallnacht*, the Night of Broken Glass, named for the shattered shards that littered the streets after Jewish-owned stores, homes and synagogues were looted and destroyed by the Brownshirts, the Nazi paramilitary force. The German authorities did nothing to stop it.

That night, atrocities were being committed by civilised Germans all over Leipzig, all over the country. Nearly every Jewish home and business in my city was vandalised, burned or otherwise destroyed, as were our synagogues. As were our people.

It wasn't just Nazi soldiers and fascist thugs who turned against us. Ordinary citizens, our friends and neighbours since before I was born, joined in the violence and the looting. When the mob was done destroying property, they rounded up Jewish people – many of them young children – and threw them into the river that I used to skate on as a child. The ice was thin and the water freezing. Men and women I'd grown up with stood on the river-banks, spitting and jeering as people struggled.

'Shoot them!' they cried. 'Shoot the Jewish dogs!'

What had happened to my German friends that they became murderers? How is it possible to create enemies from friends, to create such hate? Where was the Germany I had been so proud to be a part of, the country where I was born, the country of my ancestors? One day we were friends, neighbours, colleagues, and the next we were told we were sworn enemies.

When I think of those Germans relishing our pain, I want to ask them, 'Have you got a soul? Have you got a heart?' It was madness, in the true sense of the word – otherwise civilised people lost all ability to tell right from wrong. They committed terrible atrocities, and worse, they enjoyed it. They thought they were doing the right thing. And even those who could not fool themselves that we Jews were the enemy did nothing to stop the mob.

If enough people had stood up then, on *Kristallnacht*, and said, 'Enough! What are you doing? What is wrong with you?' then the course of history would have been different. But they did not. They were scared. They were weak. And their weakness allowed them to be manipulated into hatred.

As they loaded me onto a truck to take me away, blood mixing with the tears on my face, I stopped being proud to be German. Never again.

CHAPTER THREE

Tomorrow will come if you survive today.
One step at a time.

T HE TRUCK TOOK ME TO THE ZOO, WHERE I WAS detained in a hangar with other young Jewish men. When I arrived, there were 30 or so. All night, the thugs dragged more of us in, and when they had 150, they loaded us into another truck. As we drove, the other men told me about the disaster of *Kristallnacht*, about the looting, the burning of the synagogues. I was in shock, terrified, worried about my family. At the time, none of us understood that this was only the beginning of the nightmare. There was much, much worse to come as the truck left the city, and we were transported to Buchenwald concentration camp.

The Nazi thugs had beaten me so badly that when I arrived in Buchenwald, bruised and bloodied, the commander panicked and had his guards drive me 38 kilometres to the nearest hospital. They left me there for two days, unguarded, while I recovered from my injuries under the care of German nurses. I asked one of them what would happen if I were to escape and she looked at me sadly.

'Do you have parents?' she asked.

'Of course.'

'If you were to try to escape, they would find your parents and hang them fifteen minutes after you walk out the front door.'

This put all thought of escape out of my mind. I had no idea what had become of my parents – had they escaped from Leipzig before the Nazis came? Had they found safety with a friend or relative? Or had the Nazis come for them? Had they been imprisoned elsewhere in Germany? I just didn't know, and my fear and worry kept me prisoner just as effectively as guards. When I had healed enough that I was no longer at death's door, the hospital called the Buchenwald camp and Nazi guards came to take me back.

When I was delivered to Buchenwald, I was at first relieved. I had been given medical attention and I was surrounded by other Germans, most of them civilised, middle-class professionals. I even made friends with some of my fellow prisoners. My best friend there was Kurt Hirschfeld, a young German Jew from Berlin who had been arrested on *Kristallnacht*. Because of all this, I thought I would perhaps be safe. How wrong I was.

Buchenwald was the largest concentration camp within Germany's borders. It was named for the beech forests that stood nearby, which became known as the Singing Forest for the screams that rang out from the prisoners who were tortured there.

The first prisoners were communists, rounded up in one of the first Nazi purges in 1937, followed by many other people deemed sub-human by the Nazis: political prisoners, Slavs, Freemasons and Jews.

When we first arrived, the camp was not ready for the number of prisoners it would have to hold. There were no dormitories or barracks set up, so they herded us inside a giant tent where we slept on the floor until they could work out accommodation. At one point, 1200 Czech men were housed in what had once been a stable for eighty horses. They slept five to a bunk, pushing the beds together and lying across them like sardines in a can. The conditions were so harsh that sickness and starvation were inevitable.

History looks back at the horrors of the concentration camps of the Third Reich and the images are well known – images of Jews, starved, tortured, traumatised after the inhumanity of their persecution. But when I first arrived, that was all to come. At the start, we had no understanding of what our captors were capable of. Who could have imagined it?

We could not fathom why we had been rounded up and imprisoned. We weren't criminals. We were good citizens, hardworking, regular Germans who had jobs and pets and loved our families and our country. We had taken pride in our dress and our positions in society, enjoying music and literature, and good wine and beer and three square meals a day.

Now, the standard meal was one bowl of rice and stewed meat. You could tell the important political prisoners by the heavy chains they were forced to wear, binding their ankles to their wrists. These chains were so short and heavy that they could not stand while they ate and had to hunch over their dishes. We weren't given spoons, so had to eat with our hands. This wouldn't have been so bad if the conditions weren't so unsanitary. We had no toilet paper and had to wipe our backsides with whatever rags we could find, or with our hands. There was no proper toilet either. Instead, we had a giant pit latrine, a long trench, and we would be forced to go at the same time as up to twenty-five other men. Can you imagine the sight? Twenty-five men – doctors, lawyers, academics – carefully balancing on two planks of wood to relieve themselves over a pit full of human waste.

My friend, how to explain how surreal and horrible this all was to me? I could not understand what had happened. I still don't understand it, not really. I don't think I ever will.

We were a nation that prized the rule of law above all else, a nation where people did not litter because of the inconvenience it caused to have messy streets. You could be fined 200 marks for throwing a cigarette butt out your car window. And now it was acceptable and encouraged for people to beat us. We would be beaten for very minor infractions. One morning, I slept through the bell for headcount and was whipped. Another time, I was thrashed with a rubber baton for having my shirt untucked.

Each morning, the Nazis would play a terrible game. They would open the gates and let two to three hundred people go. When the poor people had made it 30 or 40 metres, the machines guns would start, gunning them down like animals. They would undress the bodies, put them in body bags, and send them home with a letter saying, 'Your husband/brother/son tried to escape and died in the process.' The proof would be the bullet in his back. This was how the bastards solved their over-population problem at Buchenwald.

Otto von Bismarck, the first chancellor of unified Germany, once warned the world to watch out for the German people. With a good leader, they were the greatest nation on Earth. With a bad leader, they were monsters. For the guards who persecuted us, discipline was more important than common sense. If a soldier is told to march, they will march. If they are told to shoot a man in the back, they will do it, and never question if it is right or wrong. The Germans made a religion of logic, and it turned them into murderers.

Quickly, many saw death as a better alternative to life in Buchenwald. I knew a dentist, Dr Cohen, who was beaten so badly by the SS that his stomach ruptured, and he began to die a slow, agonising death. He paid 50 marks, about a week's wages, for a smuggled razor blade. A man of science, he calculated exactly which arteries he needed to cut and how long it would take him to die. He made a plan to sit on the lavatory, right in the middle, at exactly the right time so that he would have seventeen minutes before a guard came, which is how long he'd calculated he would need to lose enough blood to die. Then he would fall into the toilet so they couldn't pull him out, or they would wash him off, sew him up, punish him, and tell him, 'You die when we want you to die. Not before.' This poor man succeeded in his grim mission – he escaped the Nazis on his own terms.

This was Germany, 1938 – completely transformed, no morals, no respect, no human decency. But not all the Germans were without reason.

One of the first Nazi soldiers I saw after coming to

Buchenwald was a familiar face, a man from my boarding house when I was studying engineering. His name was Helmut Hoer and he had always been friendly to me, back when I was living under the assumed identity of Walter Schleif.

'Walter!' he said, 'What are you doing here?'

'I'm not Walter,' I told him. 'I'm Eddie.'

I spat on his shoes, told him how shocked I was. Who I really was. That I could not believe this man, once a friend of mine, a good man, was now a guard for the SS.

Poor Helmut – he didn't know I was Jewish. I have never seen someone so confused and so panicked. He told me he wanted to help me, that he couldn't let me escape, but he would do what he could. He went to the commander of the camp, and told him that I was a good man, and that I was an exceptional toolmaker. The Nazis needed toolmakers.

The Third Reich was preparing for *Der totale Krieg*, total war against the world. In total war, there was no difference between soldier and civilian, guilty and innocent, military and industry. German society was being entirely reorganised to make weapons of war, so anyone who had any expertise in machinery or manufacture was a potential asset to the war effort. Not long after Helmut vouched for me, I was summoned to the commander's office. They asked me if I wanted to work for them.

'Yes.'

'For the rest of your life?'

'Yes.'

It cost nothing to say yes. The Jews had become the scapegoat, as they had been time and time again over the centuries, but the hunger for money and productivity in the Third Reich still overpowered the insanity of pure hatred. We were in prison, but if the German state could make money out of us, then we were still useful to them.

They made me sign a contract of employment and a statement to say that they looked after me well, they had fed me and that my time in the camp had been comfortable, and then they made plans for my transfer. As part of the deal, they allowed my father to pick me up from Buchenwald and take me home to spend a few hours with my mum, and then escort me to the factory, where they would put me to work until the day I died. After *Kristallnacht*, he and my family had returned to Leipzig, and had been quietly waiting for times to get better. Although they wanted to flee Germany, they would not leave me behind.

My father was overjoyed, having found an opportunity to win my freedom. On 2 May 1939, at 7 am, my father picked me up in a hired car. I left Buchenwald, six months after I'd arrived.

My friend, can you imagine how good it felt to leave?

For my father to drive up to the gates of Buchenwald and embrace me? To climb into the passenger side and drive off to freedom? This was paradise, a feeling of freedom and the end to persecution.

I would remember this feeling often in the years to come, and remind myself that if I could survive one more day, an hour, a minute, then the pain would end and tomorrow would come.

CHAPTER FOUR

You can find kindness everywhere,
even from strangers.

M Y FATHER WAS SUPPOSED TO TAKE ME TO an aeronautical factory in Dessau where I had been requisitioned as a toolmaker. Instead, we turned the car around and drove straight to the border. We were going to escape the country – this might be our one chance. My mother and sister, still in Leipzig, would follow and we would all reunite in Belgium.

We had no luggage and little money as it would have been too large a risk if the Germans were to search the car and find us packed for a trip. We drove to the border town of Aachen, where we met a people smuggler in a restaurant who we paid to escort us from Germany into Belgium. We left the hired car behind and, with a small group of other escapees and the smuggler at the wheel, we drove through the night along a dark forest road in order to reach a lonely and sparsely populated part of the border. The smuggler had promised to take us into Belgium, but instead took us to the Netherlands, where we gathered in the dark with seven other refugees on the side of a road. The roads of the day were the envy of Europe – wide, well-built, and elevated a metre and a half above a drainage ditch that ran alongside. We huddled in that ditch, waiting for the opportunity to run. The smuggler warned us that soon a truck would pass by with a searchlight mounted on the back. We were to wait until the truck passed and then run as quickly as we could before the light could swing back to find us. Once we were across the border, we would have to move as quickly as we could until we were ten kilometres away from the Netherlands. After that, legally, we would be in Belgium where the Nazi regime had no power to capture us. Many of the Jews who had fled to the Netherlands were subsequently returned to Germany, while Belgium was accepting more refugees trying to escape Germany and the worsening persecution.

I was nervous, sweating and very worried that we would not make it, but my father was calm. He told me to stay close and that he would grab me if anything went wrong. Sure enough, before long the truck came rumbling through the night, making a great deal of noise. The light dazzled my eyes, but I felt a hand grab the back of my belt, the fingers keeping firm hold. It is my father, I said to myself, scared of losing me in the rush. We waited and, seconds after the truck had passed, I began to run along with the group, making the safety of the ditch on the Belgian side of the road seconds before the searchlight swung back. I realised then to my horror that the person hanging onto my belt was not my father but one of the women in the group. My father was behind us. He had stopped to help a woman up the embankment and was only halfway across the road when the light swung back and spotted him. He had to make a split-second decision – turn back to the Netherlands and possible capture or race for Belgium and endanger those of us who had escaped. He made the brave choice to turn, and disappeared back into the Netherlands.

I was very worried, but I had no choice. I had to keep moving. We'd made a plan to meet at a hotel in the tiny Belgian village of Verviers if we got separated. I took a room there and waited anxiously for a night and a day before my father turned up, badly injured.

He had been caught by the gendarmerie (Belgian police) trying to cross the border again and they had beaten him. He had very little money but offered the police his platinum cufflinks if they would let him go. The chief inspected the cufflinks and told him that they weren't platinum at all, just enamelled, and handed him over to the Gestapo. He was under custody on a train back to the camps when he broke free, pulled the emergency brake to stop the train and escaped. That night, he was able to successfully cross the border and we were reunited at the hotel.

The next morning, we travelled to Brussels where my family had rented an apartment right in the heart of the city. It was a very nice apartment, comfortable, with room enough for my mum and sister. But they did not come. They were supposed to make the same border crossing together, but they had been arrested and were in gaol in Leipzig. When we called to talk to them, the Gestapo answered the phone. They told me that if I didn't come back right away, they would kill my mother.

What to do? How could I leave my mother behind? How could I put her in such danger? I asked if I could speak to her for one minute, and the second she was on the phone, she cried out, 'Don't come back! It's a trap! They'll kill you!' And the line went dead.

I didn't know until later that the Gestapo officer took the phone and bashed my poor mother in the face with it, shattering her cheekbone. It never healed right, and for the rest of her life she suffered a sunken cheekbone of angry, puckered flesh which she had to cover with a patch.

Can you imagine the horror I felt? I rushed out in fury and panic, ready to travel back to Germany right away. I insisted that I could not let my mother suffer. My father forbade me, and we fought bitterly about it. He was convinced that if I handed myself over, I would soon be dead.

'You're not going!' he told me in tears. 'I cannot lose you too.'

Mum was in gaol for three months before she finally managed to negotiate the release of her and my sister. The minute she got out, she took my sister on the train to Aachen, on the border with Belgium, where they met the people smuggler who had got my father and me over the border. We were all to be reunited in Brussels.

But by the time they arrived, I would already be gone.

Two weeks.

I was free for two weeks before I was arrested by the Belgian gendarmerie. Not, this time, as a Jew, but a German who had crossed the border illegally. I could not believe it. In Germany, I was no German, I was Jewish. In Belgium, I was not Jewish, but German. I could not win. I was arrested and put into the Exarde refugee camp with 4000 other Germans.

This time, I was surrounded by all kinds of Germans, most of them refugees from Hitler's Germany – socialists, communists, homosexuals, people with disabilities. The conditions in the camp were, if not pleasant, remarkably civilised after the savagery and sadism of Buchenwald. We had certain freedoms and could wander as far as 10 kilometres away as long as we returned in good time. We had our own beds, and three meals a day – each morning, bread and margarine with marmalade or honey. They fed us well, and it was possible to live a decent sort of life. The hardest thing was having no contact with my family. They were in Belgium, but I had no way to contact them without alerting the authorities to their location.

I made an application to the Belgium government, pleading my case. 'I don't know why you are putting me in a camp because I'm German. I'm not with the Nazis, I've never collaborated with the Nazis, but I ask your permission to perfect my French. I'm willing to teach the young people of your country mechanical engineering.' They accepted and gave me an identity card which allowed me to take the train every day to Ghent, a beautiful old city in the Flemish region of Belgium, about 20 kilometres away from the camp, which meant I needed special permission to visit. Each morning at 7 am, I would walk to the police station, have my identity papers stamped, and then travel to the university to teach. I was made an instructor in their mechanical engineering faculty. There was time enough for me to learn Flemish, improve my French and become good friends with many at the university.

I also made friends with some of my fellow prisoners.

And can you believe it, my friend from Buchenwald, Kurt, was there! He had escaped the camp and made his way to Brussels, where he had been arrested as a refugee. He didn't work, but every night we would meet and spend time together. We also befriended another Jewish man, Fritz Lowenstein, a gifted cabinetmaker who encouraged me to make the most of the situation and put my knowledge to work.

We stayed there almost a year – until 10 May 1940, when Germany invaded Belgium and it became unsafe for the refugees to be there. Among the prisoners were a number of political refugees who had been high-ranking German politicians opposing the rise to power of the Nazi party. After the fall of the Third Reich, they had planned to return and rebuild the shattered remains of German democracy. One was a very kind and smart fellow named Artur Bratu who had been a politician in the Social Democratic Party of Germany during the Weimar Republic.

He was a very calm and inspiring leader, and even though he was a political exile, he had an inextinguishable hope that he would one day return to Germany and help to restore sanity. I thought to myself, I will follow this man, whatever happens. He is a survivor.

Plans were made to evacuate us to Britain. A refugee ship was organised to take us from the Belgian port of Ostend. Unfortunately for us, the Belgian official in charge of the evacuation was a collaborator and wanted us to fall into the hands of the Nazis. He made sure that by the time we got to Ostend, the ship had left without us. At a loss for what to do next, Bratu, now our default leader, decided to take us to Dunkirk, almost 50 kilometres away. The French port city would have ships and a possible avenue of escape from the European mainland. We began walking along the coast to France in the hopes of finding rescue.

The journey to Dunkirk took about ten hours. While we were walking, German troops were streaming across France and Belgium – it had taken the German Panzer tanks a little more than two weeks to crush the Allied armies and drive them into retreat, and we arrived right in the middle of the legendary evacuation of Dunkirk. The *blitzkrieg* had demolished Allied military resistance, and now their troops were trapped on Dunkirk beach, waiting for rescue by a civilian fleet while being heavily bombed by German troops.

Many thousands of Allied soldiers were lying dead on the ground, and the air was full of gunfire and explosions. The soldiers were holding the Germans back with small arms fire while they were slowly evacuated, one small ship at a time. They had only 12 hours to get the soldiers who could walk off the beach; the dead had to be left behind. Our ragged group of a dozen or so begged to be let on a ship, but the captain refused.

'We can only take English soldiers,' he said. 'I'm sorry.'

Fritz had an idea. He found the body of a poor English soldier who was about his size and took his uniform off. He was able to slip past the English officers and get on a boat to safety. I tried to do the same thing. A young English soldier had been shot and had died resting on a log. Feeling very ill, I unbuttoned his jacket to borrow it. When I moved his body to undress his lower half, I found that the bullet had exploded through his stomach and I couldn't do it; I just couldn't bring myself to take this poor boy's clothes. It was one thing to improvise and be resourceful, but another to steal this poor dead soldier's dignity, the last thing, the only thing that the war had not taken.

We were caught right between the German and Allied armies – heavy guns getting closer, German bombers screaming overhead. In the chaos of the evacuation, I lost the group and so, suddenly alone, I decided to travel on foot to the south of France, where there might be another avenue of escape. I was joined on the road by thousands of refugees, a long line that seemed to stretch as far as France.

I walked all the way to the south of France.

For two and a half months, I was walking sun-up to sundown. It took me a long time because I kept to the back roads, walking through little villages, where there was less chance of running into Nazi soldiers and SS officers on the lookout for escaped prisoners.

I must tell you, I have never experienced so much kindness from strangers as I did in the small villages of France. I was sleeping rough – in doorways and in hidden places in public areas – and waking up very early to start walking again so I wouldn't make the authorities suspicious. The Nazis held power everywhere in France now, with collaborators working hand-in-glove with the occupying forces. It was often still dark when I started walking, but the villagers would see me and call out in French, 'Have you eaten? Are you hungry?' And they would invite me in to share their breakfast. These were people who had very little themselves, poor farmers who were already suffering from the hardships of the war, but they were willing to share everything they had with me, a stranger – and a Jew. They knew they were risking their lives helping me, and still they did it. Even when these villagers were hungry themselves, they would slice up their bread and make me take some with me. Not once did I have to beg for food or steal to survive. After the war, it would emerge that out of all the countries in Europe, the

French people were among the bravest and most righteous in hiding and protecting Jews and other persecuted minorities.

In Lyon, there were so many refugees that the roads were closed and I couldn't go any further. By then, exhaustion and lack of food had worn me down, and I was sick and growing very weak. I went to a public restroom to clean myself up. The custom in those parts was to pay one franc to a washroom attendant, who would provide you with a towel and clean the facilities after you had used them. I paid my franc and the attendant took my coat and showed me the sparkling clean restroom. I had only just sat down on the toilet when the door was kicked open again, and a group of angry women who had been passing by dragged me out with my trousers still down, kicking and spitting at me, yelling, 'Parachutist!' Germany had been dropping spies all over Europe via parachute. They would parachute in behind enemy lines with a radio, and then radio instructions to bombers on where to aim their ordnance.

The woman had gone through my pockets while hanging my coat and found my German passport. She thought I was a German saboteur spy! My luck was not good that day. As it happened, a French policeman was walking past and came in to see what all the commotion was about. I was arrested again, this time as a German, not a Jew.

I was sent to a concentration camp called Gurs near Pau, in southwest France. It was very basic, very primitive. It had been built in a rush in 1936 for the Spanish people escaping the Spanish civil war. But again, I had a bed and three meals. I spent seven months there and might have lived out the war in quiet but dignified misery if it weren't for a cruel twist of fate. Hitler was increasingly obsessed with Jews in Europe, particularly those who had escaped to territories that he had since invaded. Many of us were highly educated professionals, doctors, scientists – the people Hitler needed to advance science and industry in his state. And he wanted us back.

The collaborator Head of State of Vichy France, Philippe Pétain, wanted to free skilled French prisoners of war, and the foreign Jews across France were his bargaining chip.

I didn't know what was going on until the commander of the camp called me into the office. He said I was going to be sent away along with the rest of the Jews. Until that day, I didn't even know there were other Jews in the camp. Of the nearly 15,000 prisoners, 823 of us were loaded into trains, 35 people to a wagon. As we were moved onto the platform to board the train car, I asked one of the guards where the train was going, and he told me we were heading to a concentration camp in Poland. This was the first time I heard the name Auschwitz.

CHAPTER FIVE

Hug your mother.

I DID NOT KNOW ABOUT AUSCHWITZ THEN; HOW COULD I? How could any of us know such a thing was even possible? But I understood enough about the Nazis to know I could not go back to one of their camps. Standing in comparatively safe French territory, on a French train platform, with French guards and French engineers, I determined to escape.

I knew from my training that the engineer on every French train station had a small toolkit with a screwdriver and a shifting spanner. While the guards were distracted, I stole these and hid them inside my jacket. I went to the train driver and asked him in French how long it would be until the train entered Germany. It would be nine hours. I had nine hours to get out, after which there would be no hope of freedom.

Once the train car started moving, I set to work.

I unscrewed all the bolts from the floor but didn't realise the floorboards of the train were interlocked. Each piece of wood had a tongue and a groove holding it in place, so it was impossible to remove even after the bolts were taken out. However, I still had a good screwdriver, and started chipping away at a floorboard to loosen it. It took me almost nine hours of hard work to loosen two floorboards. By then, we were maybe ten kilometres away from the border crossing at Strasbourg. There was no more time.

Nine of us, those who were very skinny, desperately wriggled through the hole in the floor and escaped. We crawled through like spiders, clinging to the bottom of the train car. I hung with my fingertips for dear life until I could tell from the motion of the train and the lights visible up ahead that we were close to entering Strasbourg, where we would surely be captured. I yelled for the others to let go and we dropped onto the railway tracks, lying as flat as we could against the sleepers. We covered our heads with our hands as the train roared overhead, aware that loose chains on the bottom of the carriages could have caught us and split our skulls like melons.

Then the train was gone and the open sky was above my head.

For safety's sake, we decided to split up and go in different directions. It wasn't long before I lost the others in the darkness. I never saw any of them again. Getting my bearings, I figured out which direction would take me towards Brussels, more than 400 kilometres, and started on my way. It was too dangerous for me to walk into a station and try to board a train – I would surely be arrested. Instead, I decided to stand just outside the station and jump onto the first train heading in the direction of Brussels. I had to be sure to jump off the train again before it pulled into each station – soldiers were searching the trains at every station, and I would not survive. In this way, hopping on and off trains in the dead of night, it took me close to a week to travel back to Brussels.

I went first to the beautiful apartment my parents had been living in and called up, but the man living there knew nothing of them. I made contact with a family friend, DeHeert, who I hoped could tell me the whereabouts of my parents. He and my father had been friends for years, and he often used to visit us when I was a child in Leipzig. Each year, we would exchange Christmas cards. He was a police commissioner in Brussels, and because of his connections in law enforcement and because my father trusted him, he was part of our contingency plan. My father had made an arrangement with him that if my family were separated, DeHeert would always let him know where the other members were.

I remembered the police district he worked in, so I knew how to find him. I met him at his station, and he took me out to a café where we could talk privately. I learned that my parents had left the nice apartment and gone into hiding outside of Brussels. My sister Henni was there too, safe and sound. Or, at least, as safe as they could be in a German-occupied country. But then, where else could they go? The Nazis were everywhere.

DeHeert gave the address, and we were reunited. They'd found a hiding place in the attic of Mr Toher, a very old gentleman, in his late nineties, who ran a boarding house. He was a kindly Catholic man and had no idea about the state of the world. He was too old to get out much and didn't understand it was illegal to harbour Jews in his attic. I don't think he even knew what a Jew was.

So we had sanctuary, but my parents were not in good shape. My father's beating at the hands of Belgian police over a year before had been worse than he'd let on. He had difficulty walking and stomach troubles for the rest of his life.

The attic had two cramped rooms and, while comfortable enough, it was far from the life we had once led. There was no bathroom in our apartment – we had to go one floor down in the middle of the night when the other boarders were asleep. But my father did his best to make it feel like home. He found lovely furniture and made it as bright and cheerful as he could, given the circumstances.

For two months, my two aunts, my mother's sisters, lived

with us. They were safe for a while, but one day they went back to our old apartment in Brussels to check the mail, and the Gestapo were waiting. We never saw them again. They were arrested and put on the Twelfth Transport, bound for Auschwitz. They didn't even survive that long. Their train was diverted along the way and sealed in a tunnel, where it was allowed to fill with fumes, killing every man, woman and child aboard. Nobody knows what happened to them after that – the records and witnesses are lost to history. Where my murdered aunts are buried or their ashes scattered, we will likely never know. This breaks my heart still, after all these years.

It was very dangerous to be outside. We had to be afraid of anybody who might denounce us. I didn't like to leave in the daytime – my hair was dark and, to the wrong eyes, this would have marked me as a Jew. My sister, at least, was very beautiful with fine features and light hair. She looked 'German' enough to be able to go out for a little while in the day to try to find food for us. But it was still very hard. We had no money, and worse, we had no ration stamps.

The war had created shortages of everything. It was impossible to buy food without stamps, and impossible to get stamps without Belgian citizenship. In desperation,

I walked to dozens of factories looking for work, but no one would give me a chance without papers. Finally, a man named Tenenbaum – a Dutch name – gave me a job. I would maintain and repair the machinery in his factory at night when nobody else was around, and he would pay me in cigarettes. The work had to be done in absolute secrecy, in the dead of night. A curfew was in effect – anybody found on the street after dark without papers would be shot on sight. I would walk to the factory once night fell, being careful to avoid patrols. In the factory was a small hidden capsule which I could open a certain way. Each night, Tenenbaum would leave notes about which machinery needed repairing. I would work all night sometimes, racing against the clock to get it done by sunrise. With the curfew in effect, there could be no lights on in the factory, so I covered all the windows with black paper so they couldn't see there was anyone inside. Then I would walk home with my pay in a backpack – ten cartons of cigarettes.

But what on Earth was I going to do with cigarettes? We needed food! I visited more than a hundred shops and businesses looking for someone who would buy the cigarettes, and I was lucky enough to meet a kind woman who ran a restaurant, Mrs Victoire Cornand, who agreed to sell the cigarettes for me and buy essentials. Each night, on my walk back into Brussels, I would leave the cigarettes in her dog kennel. She would then go out and sell them on the black market, and when I returned the next day, I would find groceries: potatoes, bread, butter, cheese. No meat though. My family had no meat for a whole year. There was nowhere to find meat anywhere, even for Mrs Cornand, who had enough stamps. But this was enough. It kept me and my family alive and safe for months.

On my way home one night, I heard a car coming and I had to go into a doorway to hide. I made it just in time, but I didn't realise I had company until it was too late. A giant St Bernard hound had been asleep in the doorway – I don't know how I missed him, he was huge, with a head like a horse – and he bit me very badly, tearing a huge chunk of flesh out of my backside. That dog could have easily killed me but, luckily, he was happy with just a bite before running off down the street. I limped home, where I didn't tell my parents what had happened – it would only worry them. It was risky to go out in the day as well, but I would have to get treatment. In the morning, I found a chemist who would give me a syringe and a tetanus shot, then I gave myself the necessary injection. Then I went to work as usual the next night, where I ran into my boss, who was working late. I told him what had happened and he laughed, and said, 'Better a bite on the bottom than a bullet in the head!'

We had to think about safety all the time. My father covered the entrance to one of the rooms with a false wall and put planks outside the windows so we could run from one roof to the next if the police came. There was another Jewish family with three young children hiding in the building next door. One day, the parents were taken and the children had nowhere to go, and so we took them in as well, two boys of twelve and thirteen, and their sister, only ten years old. And now they were orphans. My mother treated them as though they were her own children. Her kindness was inexhaustible.

Not long after this, I had a wonderful surprise – Kurt Hirschfeld was in Brussels! He had made his way back after escaping French custody. From that moment, we were like brothers. He was not living with us, but he came many times for Friday dinner, travelling after dark, steering clear of patrols. He lived with a cousin who had an English wife, and we were able to spend a lot of time together in the evenings before I went to work. By then, he didn't have much family – his parents had already been killed in Berlin. My mother loved Kurt and took him in as if he was another son.

Sometimes now, when I am lying in bed at night, I look back and think that this was the best time of my life. I cherished this time with my whole family together in that attic. It was cramped and sometimes uncomfortable, and I was working my fingers to the bone just to subsist, but we were together. This was the life I had dreamed of all those lonely days while I was living my secret life as Walter Schleif, and then in Buchenwald. As a frightened, lonely young man, this was all I ever wanted. And for a few wonderful months, this dream came true.

Eleven months passed this way. Then, one day, Kurt disappeared. I feared the worst, that he had been denounced and arrested by the SS. I was very worried for him, but as it turned out, I didn't have long left in Belgium either.

One evening in the winter of 1943, my family was arrested just after I had left for work. The Belgian police raided our apartment and took my parents and sister into custody. They might have run but they had very little time, so they used it to hide the small children behind the hidden wall. The younger boy had a cold, so my father gave him his handkerchief to bite on so he wouldn't sneeze and alert the guards.

The police knew that I would be back, so the bastards waited for me all night long. I came home at ten past three, and there were nine policemen waiting for me in the dark, half-asleep. I insulted them, I shouted at them. 'You are traitors! You will be sorry.' It didn't help. They took me to the headquarters of the Gestapo in Brussels. My family were already there. I was put in one cell with my father, and my mother and sister were in another. But there was a small miracle – even though the police waited all night in the apartment, they never found the children. They were able to go on living. Another Jewish family took them in, and they were kept safe all through the war. Many years later, I would be reunited with them – they lived long, happy lives, one in Belgium, the others in Israel. And all thanks to my father, whose courage and quick-thinking saved them.

We were moved as a family to a transit camp in Malines, Belgium. There, they corralled groups of Jews together, waiting for a critical mass before sending the train from Belgium to Poland. The Germans were horribly efficient in their methods, and made sure that every train was at maximum capacity of 1500 people, ten carriages each with 150 people on board.

We were very worried as we waited in the cold. Although I had experienced a German concentration camp first-hand, and thought I had some idea of the nightmare ahead of us, I had no idea just how bad it would be. But then something happened that I could not believe. I saw somebody dancing with excitement and trying to get my attention from across the station, and thought my eyes were playing tricks on me – Kurt! He'd been stopped by police after curfew in Brussels and found without papers and without 100 francs on his person, enough to have him arrested under anti-vagrancy laws. I could not believe there were so many ways a person could be arrested: a Jew, a German, a vagrant! This had been a few weeks before, but they'd been keeping him in this camp until they'd rounded up 1500 Jews for deportation. A terrible circumstance, but it was wonderful to see him again.

Before long, the Nazis had rounded up their required 1500 souls and began loading us into wagons – men, women, little children. We were packed in like sardines, shoulder to shoulder. We could stand or we could kneel but there was no room to lie down, no room to take off our coats. Outside, it was freezing but inside it soon grew unbearably hot in the stale air.

The journey was nine days and eight nights. Sometimes the train would run fast, sometimes at a crawl. Sometimes it would stop completely for hours on end. There was no food and very little water. The carriage was supplied with one 44-gallon drum of water which was to last all 150 of us through the journey. Another 44-gallon drum was provided to use as a toilet, and all of us – man, woman, healthy or sick – had to use it in front of everybody else.

The water was the real problem. A person can survive a few weeks without food, but not without water. My father took charge. From his pockets – to this day, I have no idea where he found them – he produced a little collapsible cup and a Swiss army knife. Using the knife, he cut up a sheet of paper into 150 little squares. He explained a system of rationing. Everybody in the car would have two cups of water – one in the morning and one at night. This would be enough to survive and to make the water last as long as possible. Each person got a piece of paper when they got their first cup and, in the evening when they returned it, they would have their second. Anyone who lost their paper would receive no more water. Days passed and the air grew staler and fouler as the toilet bucket filled up and the water bucket emptied out. The hours were broken up by the twice-daily cups of water.

Soon, the water in other carriages ran out. Through the walls of the train, over the noise of the tracks, I could hear them crying out, one woman shouting, 'My children are thirsty! They need water! My gold ring for water!'

After two more days, they fell silent.

By the time we arrived at our destination, as many as 40 per cent of people in the other carriages had died. In our car, only two people died. Thanks to my father, the rest of the people in our carriage survived. At least, until they reached Auschwitz.

–

It was February 1944, the worst time of a bitter Polish winter, when our train arrived at Auschwitz II–Birkenau railway station and I saw for the first time the infamous iron sign looming over the barbed wire fences: *Arbeit macht frei* – work sets you free.

The ground was slippery with freezing mud, and the first people out of the carriage stumbled. The train car was raised, and there was a little jump between the carriage and the platform. We were all very weak, and some were sick, but my father and I were still strong and lingered behind to help the women, children and the elderly off the train. We helped my mother and sister down, and, while we were helping others, they disappeared into the crowd surging in front of us as the Nazis herded everyone like cattle, using batons, guns, and vicious attack dogs. Suddenly, it was just me and my father, alone in the crowd.

We were herded down the platform to where a man in a clean white lab coat stood above the mud, surrounded by SS. This was Dr Josef Mengele, the Angel of Death, one of the worst murderers who has ever lived, one of the most evil men in the history of mankind. As the newly arrived prisoners went by, he indicated whether they should walk to the left or the right. We didn't know it, but he was conducting one of his infamous 'selections'. Here, prisoners were separated into men and women, and into those who were still strong and would be sent to

Auschwitz to be used for slave labour, literally worked to death, and those who would be taken straight to the gas chambers. One side meant beginning a new life in hell on Earth, the other, a horrible death in the dark.

'This way,' Mengele said, pointing at me.

'That way,' he said to my father, pointing the other way, towards a truck that was being loaded with prisoners. I did not want to be separated from my father so I slipped from one line to the other and followed behind them. I was nearly on the truck when one of the stooges standing guard with Mengele noticed me.

'Hey!' he said. 'Didn't he tell you to go this way?' He pointed towards the entrance to Auschwitz. 'You don't go on the truck.'

'*Warum*?' I asked. Why?

The stooge told me that my father would ride on the truck because he was old, and I would walk. That was a reasonable explanation so I didn't question it any further. But if I had gone on that truck, I would have been killed. That day, Dr Josef Mengele selected 148 young men with good potential for work and sent us into the camp.

We were marched into the camp, where they made us undress and throw all our clothes into a pile. We were shown into a very small washroom, 148 of us crammed into the tiny space. I was filled with dread because I knew what was about to happen. I'd seen it happen before, in

Buchenwald. The Nazis were going to test our endurance. We would be locked in this dark, cold and cramped room for days and, when we were exhausted, the Nazis would shout things to make us panic: 'Fire!' or 'Gas!' Or they would beat one person so they would start to panic and run around, trampling other prisoners. Each of us were given a piece of paper with an identifying number on it, and we were told if we lost that number, we would hang. I came up with a plan with Kurt and two other boys I'd known at Buchenwald.

'We don't know how long we will be in this room, but we must find a corner to stand in,' I said. 'Two of us will stand guard against the wall, and the other two can sleep behind them. And then we can switch.' For three days and three nights we did this, two of us protecting the other two while every so often the Nazis would incite a panic, and all around us the crowd would surge and trample each other in the darkness. For three days and three nights, there was screaming and the smell of blood. When the lights came back on, from the 148 of us who entered, 18 were dead. One man, not far from me, had been trampled so badly, his eye was hanging from his face. I opened my hand to see if I still had my number and found that blood was running down my palm, so hard had I been squeezing the paper that the nails had pierced the skin.

The Nazis took me into a room and gave me a thin cotton uniform in striped blue and a matching cap. It had the number from my piece of paper printed on the back. And then they put my arm in a sling so I couldn't move and brutally tattooed the number into my skin so deep, it would never fade. It hurt very badly, like being stabbed with a thousand injections. They gave me a piece of paper to bite down on so I didn't bite my tongue, but that was all the kindness I would receive that day, in that hell on Earth.

Two days later, I asked an SS officer where my father had gone. He took me by the arm and led me maybe 50 metres between the barracks and said, 'You see the smoke over there? That's where your father went. And your mother. To the gas chambers and the crematorium.'

This is how I found out I was an orphan. My parents were dead. My father, the strongest, kindest man I had ever known was now just a memory, not even given the dignity of a burial.

And my mother. My poor mother. I did not get a chance to say goodbye to my beloved mother, and I have missed her every day of my life. Every night, I still dream of her, and sometimes wake up calling out to her. When I was young, all I ever wanted was to be back with her, to spend time with her, to eat the *challah* she made on Friday afternoons, to see her smile. And now, I never would again. She would never smile again. She was gone, murdered, stolen from me. There is never a day I do not think that I would give everything I have to see her just one more time.

If you have the opportunity today, please go home and tell your mother how much you love her. Do this for your mother. And do it for your new friend, Eddie, who cannot tell it to his mother.

CHAPTER SIX

One good friend is my whole world.

S UDDENLY, I HAD LOST EVERYTHING – MY family, my possessions, my remaining faith in humanity. I was allowed to keep only my belt, my one memento of a life I would never see again.

As people came into Auschwitz, the Nazis would confiscate everything they owned and take it to a special area to be sorted by Jewish slave labourers. We prisoners called this area *Kanada*, as Canada was seen as a peaceful place where all the good things in life – food, money, jewellery – were available in surplus. Everything I owned was stolen and sent to *Kanada*.

Worst of all, my dignity was stripped from me. When Hitler had written his hateful book, *Mein Kampf*, in which he blamed all the troubles of the world on Jews, he had fantasised about a world in which we would be humiliated – eating like pigs, dressed in rags, the most pitiful people in the world. Now, that had come true.

My number was 172338. This was now my only identity. They even took your name from you – no longer a man, just a gear turning slowly in a great killing machine. When they tattooed the number on my arm, I was sentenced to a slow death, but first, they wanted to kill my spirit.

I lived in a barracks with 400 Jews from all over Europe – Hungarian, French, Russian. Prisoners were segregated by race and category – Jews in this barracks, political prisoners in that. To Hitler, we were all the same, but we came from many different countries, classes, professions, all mixed in together. Many of us couldn't speak the same language, and few of us had anything in common. It was a huge shock to me, to be imprisoned with so many strangers from so many different cultures. The only thing we had in common was our Judaism, and even this meant different things to each of us. Some of us were very religious. Others, like me, rarely thought about our Judaism before it had become dangerous to be a Jew. Growing up, I had always been a proud German. This is what made what happened to us so crazy to me, why I will always ask: why? Why?

I still can't understand how people with whom I went to work, with whom I studied and played sport, could become animals like that. How was it that Hitler could make enemies of friends, turn civilised men into inhuman zombies? How is it possible to create such hate?

Auschwitz was a death camp.

You never knew when you got up in the morning if you would come back to your bed – not that we had beds. We slept on crude bunks made of hard wooden planks that measured less than eight feet across. We slept through freezing nights, ten men to a row, without mattresses, without blankets, the only warmth coming from other people. We would sleep in a row, curled up like herrings packed in a jar, because this was the only way to survive. It was so cold, eight below zero, and we were forced to sleep naked, because if you were naked, you couldn't escape.

If someone went to the toilet at night, they would have to come back and shake the first and tenth person in the line so they could move into the centre of the human pile because, if they didn't, those outlying people would freeze to death. Every night, ten to twenty people died because they were too long on the outside of the pack. Every night. You would go to sleep in the arms of the man next to you just to try to survive, and wake up to find him frozen solid, his dead eyes wide and staring at you.

Those who survived the night would wake to a cold shower, a cup of coffee, and one or two pieces of bread before walking to work in one of the German factories which relied on slave labour from prisoners. Many of Germany's most respected companies – including some that still trade today – used us for profit.

We marched under armed guard for up to an hour and a half each way to get to work. Our only protection from the snow, rain and wind were our thin uniforms, and the shoes on our feet, made from cheap wood and canvas. Every step I took in those shoes, I could feel the sharp corner of the poorly cut piece of wood stabbing into the soft part of my foot.

If someone were to trip and fall as we walked to and from work, they would be shot immediately, and the other prisoners would be forced to carry their body home. Very soon, we were too weak to carry the bodies of our friends, so we started carrying long rags from which we could fashion a stretcher. If we could not carry the bodies, the Nazis would kill us too, although they would wait until we had marched all the way back to camp so they could shoot us in front of the other prisoners to make an example. The moment you were no longer able to work, you were of no use to the Nazis, and they would kill you.

Rags were as precious as gold in Auschwitz. More precious, perhaps. You couldn't do much with gold, but you could use rags to bind wounds or to stuff in your uniform to keep warm or to keep yourself a little cleaner. I used them to fashion socks to make the hard wooden shoes a little more comfortable. Every three days, I would turn the wood of the shoe so the hard point that pressed into the skin did not wear away the same part of my foot. In these little ways, I was able to survive.

My first work detail was clearing the site of a bombed-out ammunition depot. Not far from Auschwitz was a village which had been used as a supply depot for ammunition and ordnance to be sent to the front. We were marched out to the site and picked up bits of exploded ammunition with our bare hands. It was hard, dangerous work.

I was very unhappy – the other Jews in my detail did not trust me because I was German and I soon learned to keep to myself. The exception was Kurt. My parents were dead, and I did not know if my sister had survived the selection. Kurt was my only link to my old life and a time when I was happy. I must tell you, there was nothing more important to me at that time than my friendship with Kurt. Without him, I would have succumbed to despair after my parents were murdered. We were in different barracks, but at the end of every day, we would meet, and walk and talk. This simple thing was enough to keep me going, to know that there was someone left in the world who cared about me, and who I could care about.

Kurt and I were never on the same work detail. The Germans were very precise keepers of records and had information on the locations and professions of Jewish people from all over Germany. This was part of what made them such horrible and efficient killers. Luckily for Kurt, Auschwitz had no papers on him. He came from a city on the border of Germany and Poland, and the Nazis did not have the records from that town. When they asked him what his profession was, he said, 'Shoemaker,' so he was put to work as a skilled craftsman, making shoes in a workshop right in the camp. He stayed indoors, didn't have to walk in rain and snow to work in a factory like the rest of us. We would come back, starving, blisters on our feet, and he would be safe and dry, with extra food in his belly. Every time there was leftover food for prisoners, it went first to the people in the camp – tailors, shoemakers, carpenters. The factories we worked for were supposed to feed us before we left, but there was never enough food, and when we returned to the camp, there was often nothing there for us either.

This was very good for Kurt, and often he was able to save a little of his extra food and share it with me. We were able to look after each other. This is real friendship.

There was a lot of opportunity to be found in the waste of the camp. For example, when the carpenters' hacksaws became blunt, they would throw them out. Instead of wasting that precious steel, I would collect them and grind away the teeth to create beautiful knives, and then carve polished timber handles for them. I would sell them for clothes or some food or soap, both to other prisoners – like those who worked in *Kanada* and had valuables to spare – and to civilians. In addition to Nazis, there were many civilians in Auschwitz, the cooks, the drivers. German or Polish, they were just there to survive the war like anyone else. From them, I would take commissions for custom creations. I would use the machinery at the factory to make rings for their sweethearts, engrave them with initials. I would trade a good steel ring for a shirt or a bar of soap.

One day, I found a big pot that had a hole in it and had been thrown out. I had an idea, so I patched it up and took it back to camp. I approached some of the prisoner doctors. There were many doctors in Auschwitz – maybe two out of ten of all middle-class German Jews imprisoned were some kind of doctor. Each morning, they were taken by bus to various hospitals and put to work. Sometimes they were sent to the front to work on German casualties as they came back from battle. When this happened, they were gone for days at a time. Each day, they were paid in potatoes; four raw potatoes for a day's work. But you cannot eat a raw potato – that is poison – so they would come to me! I charged one potato to boil four. This gave me a little extra food to share with Kurt. Often in the evening, I would walk to find him with my pockets full of potatoes and we would share two or three for our dinner. One night, as I was walking past the SS, one of the guards with a reputation for bullying suddenly reached out to kick me in the backside, but I turned around and he kicked my pocket full of potatoes. I had to pretend I was hurt and limp away or he would give me another one. I said to Kurt, 'I'm sorry but today, the meal is mashed potato!'

I can tell you that I would not be here today without Kurt. Thanks to my friend, I survived. We looked after each other. When one of us was injured or too sick to work, the other would find food and help the other. We kept each other alive. The average survival time of a prisoner in Auschwitz was seven months. Without Kurt, I wouldn't have made it half that far. When I had a sore throat, he cut his scarf in half and gave me one so I could recover. People saw us wearing the same scarf and assumed we were brothers; we were that close.

Each morning, we would wake up and, before work, we would walk around the blocks and talk, to keep our spirits up. We would hide little presents for each other behind a brick I had carved out in the toilet wall – soap, toothpaste, pieces of rags.

These moments of friendship and gratitude were necessary in order to survive that inhumane place Hitler had created. Many people chose to take their own lives rather than go on. It was so common there was even a phrase to describe it: go to the wire. Auschwitz II–Birkenau, a subcamp of the much larger Auschwitz camp complex, was surrounded by an electrified barbed-wire fence. To touch this fence was certain death and so, to end their lives without giving the Nazis the satisfaction of killing them, people would run to the wire and grab it. I lost two good friends this way. They went, naked, holding hands, to the wire. I do not blame them. Certainly, there were many days I would have preferred to be dead.

We were cold, we were sick. Many times, I said to Kurt, 'Let's go. What is the point of living, only to suffer tomorrow?'

Kurt refused. He would not let me go to the wire.

This is the most important thing I have ever learned: the greatest thing you will ever do is be loved by another person.

I cannot emphasise this enough, especially to young people. Without friendship, a human being is lost. A friend is someone who reminds you to feel alive.

Auschwitz was a living nightmare, a place of unimaginable horrors. But I survived because I owed it to my friend Kurt to survive, to live another day so that I might see him again. Having even just one good friend means that the world takes on new meaning. One good friend can be your entire world.

This, more than the food we shared or the warm clothes or the medicine, was the most important thing. The best balm for the soul is friendship. And with that friendship, we could do the impossible.

CHAPTER SEVEN

Education is a lifesaver.

Eddie (front right) with members of his extended family, 1932. He would be the only one to survive the Holocaust.

A teenaged Eddie with (L–R) his mother Lina, father Isidore and sister Henni.

Eddie in Belgium, 1941.

Eddie's sister, Henni, with his dear friend Kurt Hirschfeld, 1945.

Flore and Eddie on their wedding day, 20 April 1946.

Eddie and his young son Michael on their way to Australia, 1950, aboard the steamship *Surriento*.

A new life in Australia! Eddie's service station in Mascot, opened in the mid fifties.

(L–R) Harry Skorupa, Flore's mother Fortunée Molho, Eddie carrying Michael, Flore, and Bella Skorupa. The group is celebrating a fellow survivor's wedding at the Maccabean Hall, 1951.

Flore and Eddie together in Sydney, 1960.

Left: Eddie receiving his OAM from then Governor of NSW, Dame Marie Bashir, 2013.
Right: with Andre, Flore and Michael.

Speaking to thousands
of new friends at
TEDxSydney, May 2019.
Photos courtesy of
TEDxSydney and
Visionair Media.

Eddie on his 90th birthday with his grandchildren Phillip, Carly, Danielle and Marc.

Eddie with his sons Michael and Andre and their wives Linda and Eva at a Sydney Jewish Museum function, 2017.

The future generations! Above: Eddie's granddaughter Danielle with her husband Jerry Greenfield and children Zoe, Lara and Joel.

Below: Eddie's grandson Marc with his wife Rachel and children Toby and Samuel.

Eddie with his belt, the only personal belonging that wasn't stripped from him when he entered Auschwitz. Photograph by Katherine Griffiths, courtesy Sydney Jewish Museum.

M Y SECOND WORK DETAIL WAS AS A labourer in a coal mine. I don't know whether it was punishment for talking back at my first selection with Mengele, or because I was still quite strong, but they sent me deep underground to mine a coal seam. We worked in teams of seven, one of us loosening the coal with a jackhammer, the other six loading wagons to be wheeled to the surface. It was back-breaking work, very hard, and there wasn't room to stand up – we had to crouch everywhere we went. We would work from 6 am to 6 pm, and had to load six wagons in that time. We saw an opportunity for valuable rest, though, and worked very hard to fill our quota by 2 pm so we could get a few hours' sleep before going back to the hellish bunk beds. Job done, we would turn out our lamps and get some sleep.

One afternoon when we woke up, a rival crew of Polish Christians – who hated us as much as the Nazis – were stealing our wagons, replacing them with their own empty carriages. They were too lazy to work and were happy for us to be punished for it. I wouldn't stand for it, though. When we were leaving the mine, we had to walk in a line and remove our hats out of respect to the guard. I broke ranks and walked over to him to tell him what had happened. He yelled at me to get back in line, and when I opened my mouth to argue, he closed it with his fist. One of his punches caught me right on the ear, and my eardrum bled for some time.

Shortly after that, I was called to an office where I met with the commander in charge for the first time. He asked what was going on. I told him about the theft, and the beating the Nazi guard gave me.

'You want to kill us? Shoot us, get it over with. But we will be dead in a month or two because we work so hard and these other prisoners take our labour away from us.' I was dismissed and the next week, there were no more Polish men on our work detail. Everybody hugged me and said thanks, but I was not quite right for months afterward, that man had given me such a hit. I would suffer bad headaches and blurred vision for a long time. But I was happy that I stood up for my rights and those of the men I was working with in the mine. I walked away with an injury, but their lives were easier from that day on. To me, that seems like a fair trade.

Not long after that, I was summoned to a meeting with a representative of Interessengemeinschaft Farbenindustrie AG, or IG Farben, a chemical and pharmaceutical conglomerate, and told I would be put on a new work detail. The SS officers who oversaw the camp realised I had skills in mechanical and precision engineering and classified me as an Economically Indispensable Jew. These Germans – they had a special term for everything.

As long as I could work, as long as I was profitable for the Germans, I might survive. On three separate occasions, I was taken to the gas chambers and maybe 20 metres before going in, the guard saw my name, number and profession and shouted, 'Take out 172338!' Three times!

I silently thanked my father, who had insisted I learn the skills that would save my life. He'd always stressed the importance of work. He understood it was the way a person contributed to the world, that it is important for everybody to play their part in order for society to function properly. And beyond that, he understood something fundamental about the world. The machinery of society might not always function the way it is supposed to.

In Germany, it broke down altogether, but parts of it kept running, and as long as my professional skills were essential, I would be safe.

I became a mechanical engineer for IG Farben. They were one of the worst offenders against the Jews. Over 30,000 people were forced to work in their factories, and they supplied the poison gas, Zyklon B, that killed over a million people in the gas chambers.

In a way, though, I am grateful for the factories. Without them, we would be dead. More than a million Jews died in Auschwitz, but there were other camps where there was no work and nothing to hold the SS back from their dreams of complete extermination. The factory owners wanted to keep us alive and would give us injections of vitamins and glucose to keep us working. It was in their interests to keep us healthy enough to work.

The SS had different priorities. They wanted to kill us all. They were under instruction to kill as many of us as they could. Hitler had given orders for the Final Solution to the existence of Jews in the world. For the SS, the concentration camps were not only to break our spirit but to destroy us utterly. The high-ranking Nazis behind the Final Solution called the slave labour *Vernichtung durch Arbeit*. Extermination through labour. They were determined to murder each and every Jew, and they could hardly kill us fast enough. No matter how many of us they shot, stabbed, beat to death and gassed, more arrived by train every day.

At one stage, some of the prisoners fought back. Some women from Birkenau worked for Krupp, manufacturing ordnance, and they brought in explosives that they had smuggled from their jobs. Each day, the ovens stopped for two hours to cool down, and while they were cool, the operators went inside and lined them with the explosives. When men came to light them, the crematoriums were blown up. For one month, we had no crematoriums and no gas chambers. We thought this was wonderful. No smoke, no stench of death. But then they built even better ovens, and it got even worse.

As the foreman of this IG Farben workshop, I was in charge of maintaining the high-pressure air pipes which ran all kinds of machines producing supplies for the German army. I was also responsible for regulating the air pressure. I wore a sign around my neck that said that if any of the pipes were found to be leaking, I was to be hanged.

There were over 200 machines, each with a worker overseeing it, and I was in charge of all of them. I was the only one in the camp who could repair the pressure gauges that kept the machines functioning. It was an impossible task to monitor all the machines at once, so I came up with a solution. I fashioned 200 whistles and gave one to every prisoner in the factory. If they noticed the pressure starting to drop on any machine, they would blow the whistle and I would run to repair it. Although there were many different types of machines producing everything from ammunition to chemicals, the factory was built in such a way that if one stopped, all of them would, and I would be a dead man. In the year I worked there, no machine broke down, even once.

And a surprise – one of those 200 operators was my sister! She had survived selection and was housed in Auschwitz II–Birkenau, the second major camp of the complex, in the women's section. When I first saw her again, my heart broke a little. She had always been very beautiful, with fair skin and lovely, shiny hair. And now she was a prisoner, her head shaved and her prison uniform hanging off her frame which was growing gaunt with starvation. I was filled with joy to know she'd survived, but also despair because I knew how much she was suffering. It had been three months since I'd last seen her, getting off the train on the day our parents died. It was also difficult because we could never speak to each other. We could not let on that we were related because, if that relationship were known, the Nazis and the collaborators would be able to use it against us. The best we could do was a glance or a sentence as I walked by her machine. I couldn't even hug her or comfort her about the murder of our parents.

Her workstation was a very hard one. She was cutting bullets to be sent to the German army, which was very hot work and produced a lot of sparks. To reduce the risk of fire, she had to stand in a moat of freezing water, which ran from a refrigerated tank. All day long, she stood in the freezing water, a terrible thing for her health.

Mine was a difficult job too. There were so many pipes that I needed to climb a high tower in order to direct their placement – a little higher, a little lower. I had only my prisoner's uniform and it was so cold on this tower, high in the air in the freezing snow. It was often 28 below zero.

One day, I must have fallen asleep because I woke up with my head ringing. My guard had picked up a stone and thrown it to wake me up. It cut a big gash in my head and the guard rushed up, panicked, afraid he had killed me – even he would be in trouble for killing an Economically Indispensable Jew. He put a towel to my head to stop the bleeding and then drove me to a field hospital. In the end, I needed 16 stitches. As I entered the hospital, we passed a room where a neurosurgeon was operating on a high-ranking Nazi officer, removing a bullet from his head. I shouted the name of the machine he was using, and that I knew how to repair it. Four days after I arrived, while I was still recuperating, the neurosurgeon approached me. He was Professor Neubert, a leading neurosurgeon and a high-ranking SS officer. He wanted to know how I knew the name of this very specific medical machine.

'I used to make them,' I said.

'Could you make more of them?'

'Not in the *kommando* where I am. But yes.'

He offered me a job manufacturing a highly specialised operating table that was to be used in neurosurgery. For three months, I was seconded to a new work detail, working to design and manufacture the table.

My father was, as in all things, right about the importance of education and work. My education saved my life, and not for the first or last time.

CHAPTER EIGHT

If you lose your morals, you lose yourself.

THIS IS WHAT I QUICKLY LEARNED ABOUT THE Nazis. Under the Nazi regime, a German man was not immediately an evil man, he was weak and easily manipulated. And slowly but surely, these weak men lost all of their morals and then their humanity. They became men who could torture others and then still go home and face their wives and children. I witnessed how they took children from their mothers and bashed their heads against the wall. And after this, they were still able to eat and sleep? I don't understand that.

The SS would sometimes beat us just for fun. They had special boots with steel toecaps on them, sharpened to a point. They had a game of waiting until you were just past them, and then kicking you as hard as they could, right in the soft part where the buttocks joins the leg, while yelling, '*Schnell! Schnell!*' (*Hurry! Hurry!*) They did this for no reason except the sadistic joy of hurting another human being. The wounds this caused were very deep and painful, and hard to heal when we had no proper food or shelter. The only hope was to stuff the hole with rags and try to stop the bleeding.

Once, I encountered a German solider on his own and he hit me and kicked me, telling me to hurry up. That time, I stopped, looked him right in the eyes and asked him, 'Have you got a soul? Have you got a heart? Why are you hitting me? Do you want to change places with me? I'll take your clothes and food and we'll see who works harder?'

Never did this fellow touch me again. He was not so courageous or so monstrous when he was alone.

Another time, I was walking across the camp when an SS hit me and broke my nose. When I asked him why, he told me it was because I was a *Juden Hund* – a Jewish Dog – and hit me again.

This was not true, though. The Nazis treated their dogs much better than the prisoners. There was one SS guard in particular, a woman, crueller even than the others we were all terrified of. She carried a baton to beat us with and went everywhere with her big German Shepherd attack dogs. She was very kind to them, always calling them, '*Mein liebling*'. My darling. One day, one of the little children in Auschwitz told me that when he grew up, he wanted to be a dog because the Nazis treated their dogs with such kindness.

One morning, we were walking to work, ten of us in a row, telling jokes to keep our spirits up. Some of us laughed and this SS woman came over and demanded to know what was so funny.

'What do you mean, funny?' I asked her. 'There is nothing to laugh about in Auschwitz.'

She was furious and swung to hit me, but I moved a little and she missed my face, hitting me on my chest. That wouldn't have been a problem except I had hidden a tube of contraband toothpaste inside my shirt, and when she struck me, it exploded everywhere, which made us all laugh harder. She was embarrassed and made sure to take it out on me.

I was given seven lashes on my back. I was tied up to a post with my chest down and my legs secured, and two big strong men took turns lashing me. By the third, my skin had broken, and blood began to weep from the wounds. They were terrible injuries, prone to infection, and there was nowhere to go for some bandages or help. Nothing.

Then I had to stand for three hours in a cage, naked, in front of everyone passing. And every time that I fell, weak with exhaustion and cold, the walls of the cage, lined with needles, would stab me awake. They made such a mess of my back that for three weeks, I had to walk around all night and sleep sitting up, leaning with my back on another man's back. When he woke up and moved, I would fall off and have to find someone else to sleep against.

There were also prisoners who turned against their own kind, collaborators, the despicable *kapos* who the Nazis granted special favours to act as overseers of the rest of us. Our *kapo* was a real bastard, a Jew from Austria, who sent many people to the gas chamber for rewards from the Nazis of cigarettes and schnapps and nice warm clothes. He sent his own cousin to the ovens. A monstrous man.

One day, he was making his rounds and came across a group of six elderly Hungarian men who were taking a break from work to warm their hands by a burning barrel of petroleum coke. We had to do this sometimes as we had no gloves and it grew too cold for our fingers to function. He wrote their numbers down to be whipped. I knew they would not survive, but that I could – I had been whipped before – so I yelled at him to have me whipped instead. But he knew that I was economically valuable and crippling me would get him in trouble. So, he had them whipped and murdered.

He did not need to report them. He did it for his own greed. It was inhuman.

Seeing behaviour like this made me more determined than ever to stay true to myself, to keep my honour intact. It was difficult. The hunger would never leave us alone.

It sapped our morale as quickly as it sapped our strength. One Sunday, I was given my ration of bread. I rested it on the top bunk then left to get my bowl of soup. When I returned to retrieve my bread, I found it gone. Someone in my barracks, in my bunk perhaps, had stolen my food. Some people would say this is to be expected. This is survival. I disagree. In Auschwitz, it was survival of the fittest, but not at someone else's expense.

I never lost sight of what it was to be civilised. I knew that there would be no point surviving if I had to become an evil man to do it. I never hurt another prisoner, I never stole another man's bread, and I did all I could to help my fellow man.

You see, your food is not enough. There is no medicine for your morals. If your morals are gone, you go.

There were also many regular people caught up in the Nazi way against their will. Sometimes I would be working at the factory and one of the guards would whisper to me, 'What time is your toilet break?' and then when I took my break, I would find a tin of porridge and milk waiting for me in the stall. It was not much, but it gave me strength, and it gave me hope that there were still good people in the world.

But it was sometimes hard for the good Germans to make themselves known. They had to know that they could trust you. If they were caught helping a Jew, it would mean death for them too. The oppressors were just as afraid as the oppressed. This is fascism – a system that makes victims of everybody.

There was one man in particular, who worked delivering food to the prisoners at the IG Farben factory, who I became friends with. His name was Krauss and as the months passed, we got to know each other very well. He was a civilian, not a Nazi, and when he could, he would sneak me scraps of extra food. They would drive the food in, serve the gruel out of a barrel while we all lined up with our little tin cup, and then drive out the empty drums. The food was horrible, but every extra scrap I could get brought me a little closer to survival.

One time, he got me alone and told me that he had a plan to help me escape. He had made an arrangement for the delivery driver to paint one of the drums of food with a big yellow stripe. This drum would be specially modified, with a chain on the inside. When it was empty, I was to climb inside and pull down the chain very hard to seal the drum. Then the drum would be loaded onto the truck. He would put me on the rear left corner of the truck and when he had left the camp and the coast was clear, he would whistle, indicating that we were halfway between

Auschwitz and the factory. Then, I would use my weight to roll the drum off the truck as it went around the corner.

We worked very hard on the plan. On the day, I was very nervous but excited as I climbed into the drum. I held onto the chain for dear life, holding my breath, not making a sound as the drum was loaded onto the truck. I heard the truck start and felt it begin to move and, sure enough, as it was going fast, I heard the driver start to whistle, which was my signal to throw myself at the side of the barrel and roll off the truck.

The drum fell and started rolling downhill, with me inside it, going around and around like a turbine. I held onto the chain very tight as the barrel went faster and faster until it finally hit a tree and stopped abruptly. I was winded and a little bruised, but otherwise uninjured. And I was free! The plan worked perfectly . . . except for one thing. In our excitement, we had forgotten that I would still be dressed in the uniform of the Auschwitz concentration camp, with a tattoo on my arm and the same number stitched in 20-centimetre-high letters on my back. Where could I go like that? And it would soon be evening and terribly cold. I had no jacket. In the factory, we removed our coats and hung them up before we began work, so I had only my prisoner's shirt. I would need help.

I walked for a while through the woods and eventually came to a house, very isolated, with smoke coming out of the chimney. I walked to the house and knocked on the door. A Polish man answered. I could not speak any Polish, only German and French, but I asked him in both languages if he could help me, that I needed a shirt. He stared at me, didn't say a word, and then turned around and walked back down the corridor, a long entry hall with rooms on both sides. He went into the last room and I felt very relieved, sure that he would help me.

When he returned, he did not have a shirt but a rifle. When he aimed it at me, I turned around and started running. I ran in a zigzag as he shot at me, one, two, three times, more. On his sixth shot, he caught me with a lucky shot to the muscle of my left calf. I cried out but managed to escape him. I tore my shirt and made a tourniquet to stop the bleeding as I thought about what to do. I realised with horror that I would never survive if the local Polish people were my enemy as well as the Germans.

I only had one option – to sneak back into Auschwitz.

I limped back up the mountain to where I knew the latest shift of workers would be returning from their shift at the Farben factory. I made a plan. I knew that on their return, they would be making a lot of noise – hundreds of feet marching, Germans yelling, dogs barking. In all the chaos, I would hide on the side of the road and when the column passed, I would sneak in to join them.

The plan worked and I was able to join the group.

I simply walked back into Auschwitz and into my old barracks, and the Nazis never realised I had gone. My only souvenir of my escape was the Polish bullet lodged in the muscle of my leg.

Do I hate that man? No, I do not hate anyone. He was just weak and probably as scared as I was. He let his fear overtake his morals. And I know that for every cruel person in the world, there is a kind one. I would survive another day with the help of good friends.

CHAPTER NINE

*The human body is the best
machine ever made.*

BACK INSIDE THE CAMP, I RUSHED TO FIND Dr Kinderman, an older gentleman from Nice I had befriended. 'Monsieur Kinderman, I have a bullet in my leg,' I said quietly. 'Would you be so kind as to take it out?'

I was in Block 14 and Dr Kinderman was in Block 29, but he told me to meet him that night in the toilet of Block 16, the only toilet with a door. There, he would perform surgery to remove the bullet. There was no lock on the door, so I would have to hold the door closed while he operated. He had no tools but managed to find an ivory letter opener, like a tiny knife. He told me it was going to hurt like hell, but we had a plan. There was a Catholic convent near Auschwitz, not far from Block 16, and each evening the nuns would ring a bell very loudly. We waited that night until the sound of the bells rang out across the camp, as it would cover my groans of pain, and then he started working. As promised, it did hurt very much! But with just that letter opener and one big push, the doctor pulled the bullet out of my leg. He told me to lick my fingers and use my saliva as a disinfectant – with no soap and no hot water, it was the only way to clean the wound. Each night, he would meet me in the toilets and help me clean it, and sure enough, within three months, it was healed. I still have the scar, but I lived, thanks to Dr Kinderman.

I'm so sorry to say that when I tried to find Dr Kinderman after the war, I found out he had passed away. He saved my life that night and I will always be grateful. And the advice he gave me was even more valuable than the surgery. 'Eddie, if you want to survive, when you come back from work, you lay down, rest, conserve your energy. One hour of rest is two days of survival.'

Some people would come back to the barracks and run around. Some were looking for extra food, some for family and friends. Sometimes, people would find their loved ones, but there was no extra food to be found anywhere and to do so was to waste precious energy. I conserved as much as I could. I knew that every calorie spent running around was one calorie less that could be used to stay warm, to heal wounds, to keep myself alive.

This was the only way to survive Auschwitz, one day at a

time, focused on keeping your body going. The people who could not shut off everything but the will to live, to do what it took to live another day, they would not make it. Those who spent time worrying about what they had lost – their lives, their money, their family – they would not make it. In Auschwitz, there was no past, no future – only survival. We adapted to this strange life in a living hell, or we did not make it.

One day, when a transport of Hungarian people arrived, they decided to save their rations. They cut their bread in half, ate half and wrapped the other half in paper and stored it. We were furious. They didn't understand what they were doing. If the Nazis found them with hidden bread, they would beat them and say that the Jews can't even eat all the food we are giving them and use this justification to drop our rations. And rations were already not enough to keep us healthy. We were hungry all the time, skinnier every day, until we were delirious with hunger.

One man who shared my bunk, a French Jew who had been a chef before the war, would have nightmares about food. In his sleep, he would cry out about all these delicious French dishes: *vol-au-vent, filet mignon, baguette.* Nobody minded so much, except for me, because I would lie awake at night, starving, listening to this Frenchman describing all these delicious foods. In the end, one night I shook him awake.

'If you don't shut up about pastries,' I told him in French. 'I will kill you!'

Auschwitz was about survival, but it would not have been possible to survive without a good friend. Without the kindness and friendship of other people who went out of their way to help me, I would not have lasted a month.

Every morning, when the nearby convent rang the bell for prayer at 5 am, Kurt and I would meet in the showers to share our small amounts of soap. I would give one little piece of bread every month to a barber to shave our heads to keep us free from lice. We did everything we could to keep each other alive.

For nearly four months, we would have coffee every morning. It was not very good – sort of a chemical recreation of real coffee – but for those first four months, we drank it down greedily. Then one day, I smelled something strange in the cup. I went to the kitchen and said to this fellow, 'What are you putting in the coffee?'

He said, 'Bromide,' which was a chemical used to keep young men's sex drives down. You need half a cup for ten men.

'How much are you putting in?' I asked.

'Don't be silly! We cut open the tin and put the whole

thing in!' he said. Enough to chemically castrate a hundred men! So, no more coffee for Kurt and no more coffee for me. That's why I have a family today. A friend of mine in Israel survived but could never have children because he drank this coffee and it destroyed his reproductive organs.

Every day, we got weaker. And we knew that the moment we were too weak to work, we were dead. The doctor would come by the barracks regularly to inspect us and to check us for lice. He would take the shirt from one of us and inspect it. If they found even one louse, they would kill us all by sealing up the dormitory and gassing us. It was terrifying because we all had very bad lice infestations. On the morning of every inspection, we would find the person with the cleanest shirt and pick them clean of lice, and then present this one person to the doctor so we would pass inspection.

But we could do nothing about the inspection of our weight. Once a month, the doctor would come through and line us all up to inspect our backsides. The doctor would look at your buttocks and whether you had lost the reserve of fat there. If your buttocks were two strips of skin hanging down that the doctor could pinch, you were no good to them anymore and were sent to the gas chamber. Each month, many people were sent to their deaths for this reason, and we lived in fear.

Kurt and I would meet after the inspection and find the other still alive. It was a miracle, every month. Even when we were so sick, our faces stayed full enough and we lived.

I am still in awe of the human body and what it is capable of. I am a precision engineer, and I have spent years making the most complicated, intricate machinery, but I could not make a machine like the human body. It is the best machine ever made. It turns fuel into life, can repair itself, can do anything you need it to. That is why today it breaks my heart to see the way some people treat their bodies, ruining this wonderful machine we are all gifted by smoking cigarettes, drinking alcohol, poisoning themselves with drugs. They are demolishing the best machine ever put onto this Earth, and it is such a terrible waste.

Every day in Auschwitz, my body was pushed to its absolute limit, and then further. It was starved, beaten, frozen, wounded. But it kept me going. It kept me alive. And now, it has kept me alive for more than one hundred years. What a marvellous piece of machinery!

We never knew what went on in the medical area of Auschwitz. After the war, the cruel and insane medical experiments that Mengele and his doctors conducted on men, women and children behind closed doors would become known to the world, but at the time, we had only rumours. If a prisoner fell ill and was taken to hospital, chances were good that you would never see them again.

One time, I fell very ill with some kind of infection of the liver. I became jaundiced, very weak and my skin turned a sickly yellow. I was taken to a hospital ward for two weeks and Kurt was very worried about me. He didn't know if I was being treated or if I was being fed. He came to visit me, carrying a bowl of hot soup that should have been his dinner. This was in the middle of a blizzard, heavy snow and howling wind. I could see Kurt fighting his way through the storm to get to me. I could also see an SS guard following behind him. I tried to signal to him to turn back, to watch out, but he couldn't understand me, and I could only watch helplessly as the guard caught him. The Nazi took the bowl and bashed Kurt across the head with it, burning his face badly.

Poor Kurt. We iced it with snow and rushed to see my friend, Dr Kinderman. We got some cream, some bandages made especially for burns, and were able to treat Kurt's face, otherwise he would have lost all his skin. Kinderman was able to save him. He was also able to get extra medicine when my sister needed it. After a few months of standing in the freezing water, she'd developed gangrene and needed shots of a special anti-gangrene chemical.

I could arrange small, secret visits with her during quiet times at the camp. On the far end of the Auschwitz part of the camp, the fence joined onto Auschwitz II–Birkenau and, sometimes, if we were very lucky, we could arrange to meet there and talk through the fence for a few moments. This was as close as I could get to her for a long time.

CHAPTER TEN

Where there is life, there is hope.

E ACH MORNING, A BELL WOULD RING AND WE
would be moved from the barracks for a headcount. On 18 January 1945, we were woken at
3 am by the bell and, after the headcount, we were
told we would not be going to work that day. They put us
on the road to march for Germany.

The war was going very badly for the Nazis. The Russian
army was getting closer, just 20 kilometres away, and
the Nazis in charge of Auschwitz panicked. They were
very frightened that what they had done to us would be
discovered. Orders were given to evacuate Auschwitz
and its subcamps and to blow up the crematoriums. They
did not know what to do with us, so they decided to march
us from Auschwitz to other camps deeper in German
territory. This is now known to the world as the Death
March from Auschwitz. Up to 15,000 prisoners died.

Some froze to death while they walked. Others fell, exhausted. If you fell, the Nazis would put a gun in your mouth and shoot you dead on the spot, no questions. For an eternity, we marched through the snow. All night long, you could hear the guns going off as the Nazis executed us, pop, pop, pop.

It was the hardest time of my life. The temperature fell below minus 20°C. We had no food and no water. We were walking for three days. But I had Kurt with me. We reached a city called Gleiwitz and were lodged in an abandoned building of the Polish army, on the second floor. Kurt told me he could not take another step.

'Eddie, I am not going any further,' Kurt said, and I began to despair. I could not stand to see my best friend in the world shot. I searched desperately for somewhere to hide. Downstairs, in the shower, I spotted a manhole in the ceiling. I found a ladder and opened it.

I checked the ceiling space to see if it would work and found there were already three people hiding there. They scared me, but I scared them much worse – they thought I was a Nazi. Kurt crawled in with them, but the hiding place was still open. Someone had to cover it from the outside. I found a big piece of wood and covered up the hiding place, sealing Kurt inside. Before I did so, I embraced him and said goodbye. If it gave him half a chance to live, I was willing to go back and join the death march. I had the will to survive because, if I lived, perhaps one day I might see Kurt again.

We finally reached a station and the Nazis began to load us into a train to Buchenwald. We were loaded with 30 into each of the open wagons, and we began to freeze to death. Our thin prison jackets were useless against the cold. One of the men in my wagon was a tailor, and he had a plan to survive. He told us all to take our jackets off and, working steadily, he used them to make a huge blanket. So we lay under this, feet first, with only our heads sticking out for the four or five days it took to reach Buchenwald. Because of this ingenious invention, we stayed warm enough to survive.

The snow piled up. By the time the journey ended, there was almost half a metre of snow on top of the blanket. If we were thirsty, all we had to do was reach out and grab a handful. They gave us no food, but when we were travelling through Czechoslovakia, women would sometimes run up alongside the train and throw bread to us. It was not much bread – one loaf between 30 people – but even a mouthful of bread is better than none at all. And once more, it proved to me that there were still good people in the world. This knowledge was hope, and hope is the fuel that powers the body.

The human body is the greatest machine ever made, but it cannot run without the human spirit. We can live a few weeks without food, a few days without water, but without hope, without faith in other human beings? We will fail and break down. So that was how we survived. Through friendship, cooperation. Through hope. The other carriages were full of the bodies of poor souls who had frozen to death. I know because when we arrived in Buchenwald, I was ordered to unload them and take them to the crematorium. There was a handcart, a wooden box with big car tyres on it, that I could pull behind me. I began to load the bodies onto the wagon, ten at a time, and then take them slowly away. And then, as I was grabbing the legs of one dead man, he suddenly sat up and spoke! I nearly had a heart attack.

He said to me in French. 'Please, take the photo in my pocket. I was married three weeks ago, my wife is not Jewish. Tell her what happened.' I cried. He was only a boy, maybe twenty years old. He was dead before I could even get him off the train. I took the photo from his body.

Now I was back in Buchenwald, the first camp I was sent to in 1938 at the start of this nightmare. We were kept in a huge hangar as the Nazis tried to organise themselves.

I knew that from here there would be no escape – I was as good as dead. There was an SS Hauptscharführer who had become known as the Hangman of Buchenwald for his cruel and unusual torture of prisoners. He crucified priests upside down, burned prisoners with white phosphorus, and hanged prisoners from trees with a medieval torture technique. The Nazis were only getting crueller and crazier as the war deteriorated for them.

On the third night, an SS soldier came and shouted, 'Are there any toolmakers among you?'

After a pause, I put my hand up. 'I am a toolmaker.'

I knew that I had no other option. Buchenwald would mean certain death for me. Perhaps there would be a chance to live at another camp. I was moved to a small camp of only 200 people, called Sonnenburg, close to a forest. It was a lucky break. For the next four months, I had a much easier job in a specialist machine shop in Auma, 20 kilometres from the camp. I had my own private driver who would pick me up every morning, then I would work all day on the machine in an underground factory, out of the freezing cold. But I was far from free. I was chained to the machine, which was used to rectify gears. The chain was 15 metres long – just enough to move around the machine a little bit. Again, I was given a sign to put around my neck, saying that if I made seven mistakes, I would hang.

The job involved adjusting very specific parts, which required absolute accuracy. Even a fraction of a milli-metre off and the part was no good. My job was to grind them down to the perfect size. I had to be very, very careful, working from six in the morning to six at night.

There were other prisoners operating their own machines. My neighbour was close enough to talk to, but he only spoke Russian, so there was no conversation. The only human contact I would have all day was with the guard who would chain me to the machine each morning, and then come in the evening to take me back to the concentration camp. He was supposed to check on me every three hours, to bring me a ration of bread and to allow me to use the toilet, but he was a drunk and often wouldn't turn up at all. I would be desperate to go to the toilet and didn't know what to do. Finally, I opened the back of my machine and used spare rags to improvise a kind of lavatory so I could urinate into the machine, then closed it up again. If the guard caught me doing this I would surely die, but it was better to die with my dignity.

This drunken guard was unusually petty, even for an SS. He would beat me sometimes for no reason, just because he was having a bad day and had too much to drink. But then as he drove me back to the camp, he would tell me, 'Keep this a secret. If you tell anyone, I will shoot you in the back and tell everyone you were trying to escape. It will be my word over a dead Jew's.'

One day, the guard told me that the man in charge of the factory wanted to see me. I thought that I must have made seven mistakes and it was time for the gallows. I turned to the Russian man on the machine next to me and, although he couldn't understand me, I motioned that he should take my bread.

'Where I am going, I don't need bread,' I said.

The man in charge was called Goh. He was older than me, twice the age of my father, with a white coat and white hair, just like I have now. I expected to be yelled at and then hanged, but instead he spoke softly. He asked me if I was the son of Isidore, my father, and when I said yes, he started crying. He told me that he had been a prisoner of war with my father, back in the First World War. He was very sorry for what had happened, but said he was powerless to stop it.

'Eddie, I can't help you escape, but every day when you come to work, you will find extra food. It's the least I can do. But please, anything you cannot eat, you must destroy.'

And sure enough, from that day on, whenever I came to work, I would find extra food hidden in the machine. There was a little hatch on the side of my machine where specialist tools were stored. When I opened this up at the start of the shift, there would be bread, porridge with milk, sometimes salami. The food was very welcome, but by now, we prisoners who had survived were like walking skeletons. Our digestive systems were so damaged from starvation and bad food that we could barely eat. I could barely handle the porridge – I had to take it to the toilet to add extra water so I could digest it. The milk was too rich. Nor could I eat the salami – it would have killed me. I couldn't even give it to other prisoners because that would put my father's old friend in danger. So I had to dispose of it in the machine, grind it away to nothing. Imagine – starving so badly you could not eat. But the little extra kindness gave me new strength, the strength to not give up.

The kindness he showed me wasn't enough to rebuild my health because I was very weak, but it showed me that not everybody hated us. This was something perhaps even more valuable. It made me say, 'Eddie, don't give up.' Because if I give up, I am finished. If you give up, if you say it's not worth living anymore, you will not last long. Where there is life, there is hope. And where there is hope, there is life.

I was there only four months before the Russian army began to approach. English and American aircraft started to fly over the camps at night. Then they began dropping bombs. We could hear them going off, even deep underground in the factory. One night, a bomber scored a direct hit on the factory. The blast echoed all the way down to my station on the second floor and threw me to the ground. Fire would not be far behind, and the guards started to panic, running through the facility shouting, '*Raus! Raus!*' But what was I to do? I called to one of the guards, and he rushed over to unchain me from the machine. Only after we got above ground did he realise I wasn't just a prisoner but a Jew. He was furious that he'd risked his life to help me and hit me with the butt of his gun so hard, my face split open, and I would have headaches for weeks.

I was stitched up and put back to work in another part of the factory, deeper underground, working on an assembly line for gearboxes. The Nazi war machine needed gearboxes for all kind of machines – cars, trucks, tanks, artillery. I don't know where they went, but regardless, it was clear that the war was not going well for Germany.

I could hear the cannons off in the distance, the boom of Russian artillery, the ground-shaking explosions of British air-bombers. About two weeks after the bombing started, they again evacuated the prisoners, but this time, the Nazis had no plan. They would march away from the Russians, and then get too close to the Americans, and have to turn back. In the end, we were walking in circles for nearly 300 kilometres.

They did not know what to do with us. I was worried that they would shoot us. It was clear that the war was over, but we were witnesses to their atrocities. And if you are a murderer, you kill the witnesses.

Every day, we were weaker and the Nazis more desperate. Even the Nazis wanted to escape – every night, some of the guards would slip away in the darkness, abandoning their jobs.

We were marching on the road, one of the wide German roads with the ditch on either side. Every so often, a drainage pipe was cut below the road, allowing water to flow from one side of the raised road to the other. In these, I saw my chance to escape. But I would need equipment.

As we walked, I came across some wooden barrels for pickling German-style sour cucumbers, with big lids, quite thick and quite wide. I took two of these lids and carried them with me everywhere as we marched. The other prisoners thought I had gone mad. Who was this crazy German Jew, carrying these big useless bits of wood when he is already so weak? When we rested, I sat on the lids, so the guards wouldn't see me with them. Then, very late one evening, we came across an abandoned horse in a field. He was skinny, this poor horse, even skinnier than me! The commander looked at him and saw dinner. He stopped for the night and announced that we would all have soup. That night, all the guards and prisoners crowded around, waiting for their serving of horse soup.

I knew this was my one chance. Now or never.

When it was dark enough that nobody could see me, I ran from the road and jumped into the trench and then into the pipe. The pipe was half-submerged so I sank into freezing water. The water was running so fast that I quickly lost my shoes. Between the cold and the exhaustion, I felt I would sleep, so I put one piece of wood on my left side, one on the right, and let myself lose consciousness. I don't know how long I was asleep for, but when I woke up, the pieces of wood wedged either side of me were full of bullets. Thirty-eight in the right piece of timber, ten in the left. If I hadn't had those pickling barrel lids, I would have been dead, food for the rats. That is why I never saw anyone coming out of those pipes, because when we walked on, the SS would stay behind and shoot down those pipes with their sub-machine guns.

When I emerged from the pipe, there were no Nazis, no one. I was free! But in very bad shape. I took a stone and scratched at the number tattooed on my arm until it was bloody, leaving the Nazi tattoo invisible. I walked for a long time until I came to a small country house, quite similar to the one that I'd been shot at in Poland. It was very early in the morning when I knocked on the door. A young girl, seventeen or eighteen, came to the door.

'Don't worry,' I said in good German. 'I'm German, like you. I'm also Jewish. I need help. Can your father or brother help me with a pair of shoes? That's all I ask.'

She called for her father and he came to the door, a man of about fifty. He looked from my arm, where I was still bleeding, to my head, where I had a prisoner's haircut, and he started crying. He gave me his hand.

'Come in,' he said.

'No,' I said. I did not trust people. He insisted that he give me clothes – a jumper, a cap with a strong brim and proper leather shoes, which I hadn't worn in three years. I threw the striped prisoner's cap away on the spot.

The man told me to sleep in his hayshed that night, 30 metres behind the farmhouse, and he would help me in the morning. I did sleep that night in the hayshed, but early in the morning, I crept off, and walked four kilometres to the forest, where I could safely hide away from all people. I found a cave to sleep in that night, but it wasn't a good place to stay. In the middle of the night, many hundreds of bats started flying around, hitting me in the head. Luckily, I had no hair for them to get caught in!

The next day, I found another cave, one where no one would ever find me. It was so deep and dark that I couldn't find my own way out sometimes. My daily meals were slugs and snails, which I caught and ate raw. One day, a chicken came into my cave, and I leapt on it, killed the poor thing with my hands. I was so desperate with hunger, but I couldn't make a fire to cook it. I tried with sticks and stones, but I couldn't make it work. I collected some water from a creek, but that water was poisoned. I got so sick that I couldn't stand up anymore.

I decided I couldn't go on. I was so sick, I couldn't walk at all. I said to myself, if they shoot me now, they will be doing me a favour. I crawled on my hands and knees and made it to a highway. I looked up. Coming down the road, I saw a tank . . . an American tank!

Those beautiful American soldiers. I'll never forget. They put me in a blanket, and I woke up one week later in a German hospital. At first, I thought I was cuckoo, crazy, because yesterday I'd been in the cave, and now I was in a bed with white sheets and cushions, and nurses all around.

The man in charge of the hospital was a professor with a great big beard. Every so often, he would come by my bed and check on me, but no matter how many times I asked, he wouldn't tell me what my condition was.

I knew I was in bad shape. I was sick with cholera and typhoid, and malnourished, weighing only 28 kilograms. One day, a nurse named Emma came by. She put her head on my blanket to check if I was breathing and I grabbed her arm and said, 'Emma, I'm not letting your arm go before you tell me what the doctor told you.' I started to cry.

She whispered in my ear, 'You have a 65 per cent chance of dying. You'd be lucky to have a 35 per cent chance that you live.'

In that moment, I made a promise to God that if I lived, I would become an entirely new person. I promised I would walk from German soil and never come back to the land that had given me everything and then taken it from me. I promised that I would dedicate the rest of my life to putting right the hurt that had been done to the world by the Nazis, and that I would live every day to the fullest.

I have a belief that if you have good morale, if you can hang onto hope, your body can do miraculous things. Tomorrow will come. When you're dead, you're dead, but where there is life, there is hope. Why not give hope a chance? It costs you nothing!

And, my friend, I lived.

CHAPTER ELEVEN

There are always miracles in the world, even when it seems dark.

I WAS IN HOSPITAL FOR SIX WEEKS, SLOWLY REGAINING my strength. When I was better, I decided to set off for Belgium to look for my family. Before leaving, I was issued with basic refugee papers and given simple clothes – some pants, two shirts and a cap.

I made my way on foot, hitchhiking where I could. At the border, they stopped me and told me I wouldn't be allowed in because I was a German.

'No,' I said to the man at the border. 'I am not a German. I am a Jew, who Belgium handed over to the Nazis to die. But I lived. And now, I am coming into Belgium.' They couldn't argue with that, and not only did they let me in, they gave me double rations. I was allowed extra butter, bread and meat, all of which were rare under post-war rationing.

I went to Brussels, back to the very nice apartment my parents had lived in when we first escaped Germany.

It was still there, but all the belongings that they had been forced to leave behind when they went into hiding were missing and, of course, they were not there – just empty room after empty room. It was very hard to be there, knowing I would never see them again. I could find no one in my family. Before the war, I had more than a hundred relatives all over Europe. After, as far as I knew, it was only me.

I don't think I had so much joy at liberation. Liberation is freedom, but freedom for what? To be alone? To have to say *Kaddish* (a Jewish prayer) for other people? That's not life. I know many people who took their own lives when we were liberated. Many times, I was very sad. I was very lonely. I missed my mother very badly.

I had to decide what to do, to live or to find a tablet and die like my parents. But I had made a promise to myself and to God to try to live the best existence I could, or else my parents' death and all the suffering would be for nothing.

So, I chose to live.

With nowhere to go and no one to see, I spent time at a canteen set up by a Jewish welfare society. It provided meals and companionship to Jewish refugees throughout Brussels, as well as Jewish soldiers from all across the

Allied armies. What an amazing thing to see. After years of watching my people beaten and persecuted and starved into skeletons, to be surrounded by Jewish fighters, strong, battle-hardened, healthy. Soldiers from all over the world: Europe, America, England, Palestine. What an incredible sight.

Even more incredible – there, lining up for food with the rest of the men, my best friend in the world. Kurt!

Oh, that was something! Can you imagine it? This man who was like a brother to me, who had been at my side and helped me survive through hell on Earth, and who I thought had been left to die in Gleiwitz. Here he was, drinking coffee and eating cake, safe and sound in Belgium. Oh, I was so happy to see him! We embraced and wept with tears of joy.

He told me his story while we ate. He'd been in his hiding hole for only two days before he heard the heavy boots of soldiers approaching. He and the other men were terrified, thinking this was surely their last day, until they heard the soldiers speaking in Russian, and they surrendered to them. It took them a while to convince the Russians that they were harmless prisoners. They didn't speak Russian and the Russians spoke no German, and the Russians had seen evidence of Nazi atrocities all across Europe and were mad with righteous fury. But when they realised that Kurt and the others were victims, they looked after them well.

They fed them and clothed them and took them to Odessa, where they stayed safe for the rest of the war. Kurt was able to get transport from Odessa to Brussels by ship and had been in Brussels months before me.

It filled me with joy to find Kurt again. I'd been sure that he was a dead man, that I would never see him again. And now here we were, having coffee and cake. I wasn't alone in this world anymore. I was an orphan and I did not know what had become of my sister, but I had a family again in Kurt. It was a sign to keep going, to not give up. So many times in my life I had lost and then found him again – always a miracle.

Together, we went to a centre for refugees where they were supplying food and rations, but Kurt and I turned the corner and were dismayed when we saw the line, which stretched all down the street, hundreds of Jewish refugees who had lost everything.

'We will never be able to make our way if we rely on charity,' I said to Kurt. 'We must find employment.' And so we left that line and went to an employment office. We turned up and refused to leave until we had found work.

Kurt was a skilled cabinetmaker and was soon foreman of a small factory that made beautiful furniture. I found an advertisement from a man who wanted to open a factory making tools for the railway, and he needed a precision engineer. Mr Bernard Antcherl was a very kind and generous man. We went to Switzerland together and he bought all the specialist machinery we would need. Soon, I was established as the foreman of the factory and had twenty-five workers under me.

A week after we got our first jobs, Kurt and I put a deposit on an apartment, a lovely flat in the heart of Brussels. We had a car and plenty of money, but we sometimes felt bad that life was suddenly so good. People were still suspicious of Jews who seemed to be prosperous. Old anti-Semitic attitudes did not go away overnight. Sometimes, I would overhear other people on the factory floor say things like, 'Greedy Jews,' or imply that I was taking a job away from a Belgian family. This was very hurtful, especially after Belgium had taken away my whole family.

But not my whole family! A few months after I had been established in Brussels, the local Jewish newspaper printed a photo of me in a section where those who survived the Holocaust could let their scattered families know they were still alive. Soon afterwards, I found my sister Henni in a boarding house. She had survived the war after we were separated on the death march and had lived out the final months in relative safety, working on an apple farm near the Ravensbrück concentration camp. Two miracles! The two people dearest to me in the world had survived! I could not believe it. We decided she should live with me and Kurt.

I thought I had lost my family and the chance to ever have one, but now, two of my favourite people in the world were alive and by my side! I had a family after all and could begin to rebuild my life.

One evening, we were sitting in our apartment, reading *Le Soir*, the broadsheet newspaper, and saw an article about two Jewish girls who had tried to commit suicide by jumping off a bridge. They had been in Auschwitz II–Birkenau and had returned to Brussels to find their family all gone and decided to end their lives. The bridge they chose to jump off was not very high, but a barge passed regularly underneath it. If you landed on the deck, you were certain to die. The poor girls had missed and landed in the water, and were immediately arrested and taken to the mental hospital. We decided we had to do something to help them.

Kurt and I went to this hospital and asked to see the girls. We were taken to a ward where the two girls were staying along with a third young Jewish woman who had also tried to take her own life. It was heartbreaking – this hospital was no place for these women. The conditions were appalling. I went to the commissioner in charge of the hospital and told him I wanted to take responsibility for the girls.

'I have a nice apartment, I have plenty of money, I can look after these people. Please don't lock them up. The hospital is terrible. Even if you went in perfectly sane, in three months you would be quite mad.'

I managed to convince him, and so the three girls came to live with us. I opened the door to the apartment and told them, 'Look, we are two men, but there will be no monkey business. From now on, you are my sisters.' We lived together while they recovered from their ordeal in the camps. I regularly drove them to the hospital, where they had to have sulphur baths because their skin was in terrible, terrible condition. We all had to have these baths – including my sister, who was in better health than Kurt and me. Sometimes Kurt and I had to go twice a week. But soon, they were feeling much better. They weren't mad – they never had been. They had just been through hell. All they needed was a little kindness. It was something that those who didn't experience the camps found hard to understand. Giving them a home and a place to heal was a way for Kurt and me to give back, to say thank you to God for keeping us alive. In time, they were fully recovered and went out into the world to find work and lovely husbands – we have kept up correspondence ever since.

Meeting and helping those girls really made me understand my father's advice that it was the duty of the fortunate to help those who are suffering, and that it is better to give than receive. There are always miracles in the world, even when all seems hopeless. And when there are no miracles, you can make them happen. With a simple act of kindness, you can save another person from despair, and that might just save their life. And this is the greatest miracle of all.

CHAPTER TWELVE

Love is the best medicine.

I DID NOT FEEL ENTIRELY AT HOME IN EUROPE. IT WAS hard to forget that we were surrounded by people who had done nothing to prevent the persecution, deportation and murder of my people. In total, more than 25,000 Jews were deported from Belgium. Fewer than 1300 survived.

In Brussels, I sometimes felt I was surrounded by collaborators. The people who denounced my parents – I will never know who – may have been sitting at the next café table, drinking coffee. People denounced Jews out of hatred, anti-Semitism, fear or even greed. Many families were murdered because their neighbours coveted their possessions and wanted to raid their belongings after they were deported.

One day, Kurt and I were walking in the beautiful market square of Brussels and I saw something I could not believe. I turned to Kurt and pointed at a man wearing a sharp and familiar suit across the square.

'You see that man?' I demanded. 'I guarantee you that is my suit!'

'You're joking!'

'No,' I said. 'I'm following him.' The last time I had seen that suit, it had been hanging in the wardrobe of my parents' apartment.

We followed the man until he went into a café, and then I walked up and confronted him. I told him he was wearing my suit and asked to know where he got it. He told me I was crazy, that the suit was tailor-made for him. I knew he was lying. It was a very distinctive suit I'd had made in Leipzig, with knickerbocker cuffs for cycling. I fetched a policeman.

'You see this man sitting in this café? He has stolen my suit.'

'Okay,' said the policeman. 'We'll go in and ask him to take the jacket off.'

At first, the man refused but then finally relented. When he took the jacket off, sure enough, it had the brand of the very good tailor I had visited in Leipzig before the war. The man couldn't even read the German label and sheepishly agreed to return my suit. He was harmless enough – a thief only – but there were real collaborators with Jewish blood on their hands still walking around.

Once, I was out walking and ran straight into the *kapo*

from my dormitory – the Jewish criminal in charge of keeping the other Jews down. I could not believe he was alive, that he was free. I went to the police and asked for him to be brought to justice, and they told me to drop it. He had made a good marriage, to the daughter of a powerful politician in Brussels, and the police did not want to be involved.

Kurt and I considered taking vengeance into our own hands, but after seeing us, this man took precautions. He travelled everywhere in a group, as if with bodyguards, and he had two beautiful Alsatian hounds with him at all times. He, and so many other criminals and murderers, would not face justice.

Belgium couldn't seem to make up its mind about me. As a refugee, I was given permission to stay in Brussels only six months at a time. This was despite me being in charge of a factory and having signed a contract for two years!

I made inquiries and found the woman whose photo I had been given on that death train at Buchenwald, and I told her that her husband's last thoughts had been of her. She was very touched and asked me to come to dinner with her family. I arrived in a nice suit, with flowers and cakes, but the family made me feel very unwelcome.

'Oh.' The father frowned. 'You're a Jew.' I left without eating. I told the woman that we could not be friends. If we were, she would lose her family.

It was a struggle for us survivors to try to fit into Belgian society. Anti-Semitism was still very common, and our level of trust in the world was very low. We had seen horrors that no one who had not lived through it would ever understand. Even those who meant well and tried to empathise would never get it, not really. The only person who really understood what I had been through was Kurt, but we could not stay together forever. He found a girlfriend, Charlotte, a lovely woman, and they married in February of 1946.

And then, just as I feared I would never belong anywhere or with anyone ever again, I met a beautiful woman named Flore Molho. She was born into a Sephardic Jewish family in Salonica, Greece, but was raised in Belgium. When I met her, she was working for Maison Communale, the town hall of the Brussels municipality of Molenbeek, where one could collect one's food stamps during the rationing period after the war.

One day, I came in to present my double-ration card and collect my food stamps. They went to get Flore and told her there was a man with a tattoo. She had heard stories of the concentration camps, and made sure to talk to everyone she could who had lived through them, so she came to see me. I fell in love at first sight. I told her I wanted to give her everything, to take her away to start a new life, and she laughed. She went back to her office and told them that one of the freed prisoners had offered to take her abroad. They all thought it was hilarious.

She had been very lucky during the war. She was Jewish but had survived in hiding. When Germany invaded Belgium in May 1940, she was working at a local council, but the Nazis did not know she was Jewish. Life got harder, with shortages and bans soon imposed on everything from the playing of American music to the freedom to walk the streets at night, but in some ways, her life continued as normal. She still went to work and lived at home until 1942, when she was ordered to appear at the local Gestapo headquarters. She had been denounced by a colleague who wanted her job for his wife, and was told she could no longer work at the council. Then she was presented with a list of items to assemble – fork, knife, blanket – and told to report on 4 August 1942 to the former military barracks in Mechelen to be deported.

In the intervening days, her council boss learned of her intended fate and arranged through the Belgian resistance for her to be taken to France where she would assume a false identity. She took the name Christiane Delacroix – meaning Christine of the Cross, the most Christian name she could think of. For the next two years, she lived in Paris, known to everyone – except her brother, Albert, and sister-in-law, Madeleine, with whom she shared an apartment – as Christiane Delacroix.

When Paris was liberated in August 1944, she joined the crowd on the Avenue des Champs-Élysées cheering General Charles de Gaulle at his victory parade. Just weeks later, she returned to Brussels.

She did not fall in love with me straightaway. To tell the truth, she was first overcome by pity, not love. I do not blame her for pitying me! I was carrying many scars from the camps. The blow from the SS guard's gun continued to give me headaches for many years, and malnutrition meant by body suffered from terrible boils. Twice a week, Kurt and I both had to visit a specialist for sulphur baths to relieve the painful, stinking boils that erupted all over our bodies, dozens at a time.

On one of our first outings, Flore and I went to the cinema, but I had a terrible boil on my behind. I could not sit still and was in awful pain, shifting about.

'What is wrong with you? Why don't you sit still?' she whispered, and I did not know how to explain. When I got home, I asked Kurt to lance it for me so I could have relief.

But we saw each other again and in time, we fell deeper and deeper in love. Love is like all good things in life – it takes time, it takes work, it takes compassion. On 20 April 1946, we married in a civil ceremony. My boss, Mr Antcherl, who had been so kind to me, offered to walk Flore down the aisle and Flore's boss, who saved her from the camps, officiated. Flore's mother, Fortunée, cried tears of happiness. She was a wonderful woman who accepted me into her family with open arms, and immediately made me feel as though I was her own son. So I gained a wife and a mother.

Flore and I were very different people, but that is what made me so enchanted with her. I was very sensible, and methodical and I liked to work with machines and numbers. She loved meeting new people, to listen to music, cook good food and go to the theatre. When we went to a show together, she would know the works off by heart and could whisper the lines at the same time the actors did! But this is what made us such a good pair. You don't want to fall in love with a reflection of yourself! A strong partnership is with a man or a woman who is different from you, who challenges you to try new things, to become a better person.

I was a very difficult person when I was first married. I didn't want to go dancing. I didn't want to go to the cinema. I didn't want to go anywhere with a lot of people around. I had lived in fear of my life for so long that I could not stop thinking like a survivor. I had been programmed to look out for danger. My wife didn't know anything about this. Those who hadn't been in the camps didn't realise how cruel people could be and how easily you could lose your life.

I was still carrying so much pain. An old family friend in Leipzig visited our long-abandoned family home and sent me a box of recovered personal effects. When it arrived, I opened it with shaking fingers and found a trove of our photos and documents. My old legal documents; different identity cards; a book where my father had started paying insurance for me; a workbook from when I graduated as Walter Schleif. Many photos of all my loved ones who I would never see again.

It was very, very emotional. I cried. My sister wouldn't even look at it, she was too upset. It's possible to forget how much pain you carry, how much hurt there is in your subconscious, until you are presented with evidence of everything you've lost. Holding those photos of my late mother, I was struck by the thought that everyone I ever loved was gone and never coming back. And here was proof – a box of memories, of ghosts.

It was a shock. For a long time, I put it away and couldn't bring myself to look at it.

I was not a happy man.

To be honest, I was not sure why I was still alive, or if I truly wanted to live. Looking back, I feel awful for my wife. She had a challenging first couple of years with me. I was just a miserable ghost, and she was a very vivacious person, fully assimilated into Belgian society, with many friends from all backgrounds. And I was quiet and closed-off, miserable.

But that all changed when I became a father.

About a year after we married, Flore became pregnant. To make enough money to support a family, I took a job with a company that installed operating equipment all around Europe. It involved travelling to a city, installing very specific and intricate machinery for medical operations, and then spending some time training the local staff how to operate and maintain the machine. All up, it took three or four days for each job. I was in the middle of one of these assignments when I received word that my wife had gone into labour. My boss immediately hired a little plane to fly me back to Brussels – a tiny thing, not even a sealed cockpit, just the pilot and me open to the sky, with a cap and goggles for protection. We hit a storm and I thought I'd never see my wife again or meet my child. When I did finally arrive, the baby came half an hour later.

When I held my eldest son, Michael, in my arms for the first time, it was a miracle. In that one moment, my heart was healed and my happiness returned in abundance. From that day on, I realised I was the luckiest man on Earth. I made the promise that from that day until the end of my life, I would be happy, polite, helpful and kind. I would smile.

From that moment, I became a better person. This was the best medicine I could have, my beautiful wife and my child.

Our life in Brussels was not perfect but we were alive! You have to try to be happy with what you've got. Life is wonderful if you're happy. Don't look on the other side of the fence. You will never be happy if you look at your neighbour and make yourself sick with jealousy.

We weren't rich, but we had enough. And let me tell you, just to have food on the table after starving in the snow for years was wonderful. After we were married, we had a beautiful apartment with a view of Belvédère Castle. It was small, but what a pleasure to have that view. You don't need a castle of your own when you have that view, the view is the best part! And I would not want to live in the castle even if I could – too much to clean!

Other people around us had more money – *this guy drives a Mercedes, this man has a diamond watch*. So what? We did not need a car. We bought a tandem bicycle we could ride together. Of course, I looked at it and saw how it could be improved, and I put two little motors on it to do the cycling for us. When we were on level ground, I switched on one motor, and when we went uphill, I switched on two. That was enough for us.

What a miracle to be alive and to hold my beautiful baby, my beautiful wife. If you had told me while I was being tortured and starved in the concentration camps that soon I would be so lucky, I would never have believed you. In time, my wife became much more than my wife – she became my best friend. Love saved me. My family saved me.

Here is what I learned. Happiness does not fall from the sky; it is in your hands. Happiness comes from inside yourself and from the people you love. And if you are healthy and happy, you are a millionaire.

And happiness is the only thing in the world that doubles each time you share it. My wife doubles my happiness. My friendship with Kurt doubled my happiness. As for you, my new friend? I hope that your happiness doubles too.

Each year, Flore and I celebrate our wedding anniversary on 20 April – Hitler's birthday. We are still here; Hitler is down there. Sometimes, when we are sitting in the evening in front of the television with a cup of tea and a biscuit, I think, aren't we lucky? In my mind, this is really the best revenge, and it is the only revenge I am interested in – to be the happiest man on Earth.

CHAPTER THIRTEEN

We are all part of a larger society,
and our work is our contribution
to a free and safe life for all.

W E COULD NOT STAY IN BELGIUM. I WAS still technically a refugee and had to reapply to stay every six months. We were very happy there, but you cannot build a life six months at a time. Kurt had moved to Israel with his wife, and my sister moved to Australia, married and started a family.

I made two applications, one to Australia and one to France. In March 1950, I got a permit to live and work in Australia. We came to Sydney on a steamship MS *Surriento* – one month from Brussels to Paris, then Paris to Genoa, then on to Australia. We arrived in Sydney on 13 July. The trip cost 1000 pounds for us all, paid by the American Jewish Joint Distribution Committee, a Jewish humanitarian organisation also known as the Joint. I promised to pay it back and did so the moment I could.

They were very surprised, and said not many people paid the money back, but I wanted to. If they had that money, it could be used to help someone else, as I had been helped.

We arrived in Sydney on a Thursday, and I presented myself straightaway at the office of Elliot Brothers on O'Connell Street, where I was to work as a medical instrument maker. I brought my wife and child as we had nowhere else to go.

The boss laughed. 'I only need one instrument maker, not three!' he said. Then he fetched blueprints for a very complicated machine, the kind that used to be manufactured in Europe until the industry was destroyed by war.

'Oh yes,' I said. 'Very easy.' I started the following Monday.

That winter in Sydney was one of the wettest in history. From the moment we stepped off the boat until three months later, it did not stop raining. I think I saw more sunshine in Auschwitz. My wife and I were very despondent. We had seen pictures of Sydney with beautiful beaches and palm trees, and instead, it was miserably cold and wet for weeks and weeks. Everything we owned got damp. I would come home from work and hang my shirt out to dry and the moisture in the air would soak through it. We began to wonder if we had made a mistake.

But then, the sun came out, and it was lovely.

We found a room in a very nice house in the suburb of Coogee, sharing with a Polish family, the Skorupas – cousins of my father. They had never met me, had never been to Germany, but they were so kind and generous to us. Harry and Bella Skorupa were a humble and modest couple with three children of their own, Lily, Ann and Jack, who were prepared to sponsor our family and guarantee us room and board in their small Coogee house. They gave up their own beds to accommodate us and we stayed with them for several months.

Harry Skorupa was a tailor, and we became the best of friends after a terrible accident. He was asleep on a hot water bottle and his young children were trying to pull it out from under him. They each had a corner and were fighting over it when suddenly, it burst. Luckily, the children weren't hurt but Harry was burned very badly, an injury that was complicated because he had diabetes.

I drove him to hospital. The damage was terrible – all the skin on his back came off him. He needed regular treatments to recover, so each morning, I drove him to the hospital in my pyjamas, then came back home for an hour's sleep before work. On the long drive, we bonded, and soon grew very close.

Australia was good to us. Not too long after we arrived, I was at a hotel in Botany, socialising with some friends from work, and a man named Walter Rook came up to me, told me I looked new to the country, and asked if I was looking to buy a house. He said he had some land in Brighton-Le-Sands, very close to the beach, where he was building two identical houses. Would I like to buy one? I told him I did not have enough money, and he told me that this wasn't a problem – he would help me to secure credit and establish myself in Australia.

We moved in November 1950, and never looked back. Eleven months after we moved in, Flore's mother, who I loved very dearly, came from Belgium to Australia to live with us, and we built an extra room on the house to accommodate her. She, too, flourished in Australia, establishing herself as a dressmaker, and accumulating a clientele of some very glamorous Sydney women. Ladies sought her out from all over the city because there were so few European dressmakers.

In those years, Flore and I also welcomed our second wonderful child into the world, Andre. I thought I would never be as happy as the day I first held my eldest son, but Andre proved me wrong. To hold him, to watch his brother meet him for the first time, I could not believe my heart could hold so much happiness at once. It made all the suffering I'd gone through seem like a distant bad dream. What a wonderful thing, a perfect joy, to add to my growing family.

In 1956, I passed the Coogee Hotel, and they were remodelling, throwing out all the bar and panelling. I bought it all for next to nothing and installed it in my home, so I had a wonderful pub in my own home! And from the bar itself, I made two desks for my sons.

I began to think of Australia as the working man's paradise. I could not believe the opportunities Australia provided.

I decided I needed to do something that Australian society valued highly. And looking around, I saw the one thing every Australian loved – automobiles. Although I had little experience with cars, I knew I could adapt my engineering skills, and obtained a job with a company that specialised in fixing Holdens. With my affinity for machines, I quickly learned how to repair and maintain cars. Now and again I would encounter something I did not understand, so I'd take the service manual into the toilet with me to secretly learn how to fix the problem!

By the mid fifties, I had enough experience to set out on my own, and so we bought a service station in Botany Road in Mascot. We hung up a sign: 'Eddie's Service Station'.

Flore and I worked as a team – I fixed the cars, she served petrol, pumped tyres, looked after the staff, sold spare parts and kept the books. In a few years we built up the business until we employed a whole team of auto-professionals providing repairs, panel beating, auto-electrics, and even a new car showroom selling Renault vehicles.

But you cannot work with your hands forever. In 1966, we sold the garage, and I took a well-earned seven-month vacation to Europe and Israel, to visit family and friends. On my return, I became a real estate salesman employed by an agent in Bondi Beach. I studied for my real estate licence, and then we opened our own real estate agency, E. Jaku Real Estate.

We worked there until we were in our nineties, when we finally decided it was time to retire. For decades, Flore and I went into the office every day to work side by side, a great team in business, just like in life. We had the pleasure to sell or rent many people's first property to them, and even now my children will occasionally meet someone who will remember us from decades ago, and tell them we were the only honest real estate agents they ever met!

We remembered the experience of being refugees, and the importance of kindness and being helped by the Skorupas when we first arrived. To this day, we are still very close with Lily Skorupa, the daughter of Harry and Bella. So we made sure to go out of our way to help young families and those who needed a little help getting started in life.

I had learned early in life that we are all part of a larger society and our work is our contribution to a free and safe life for all. If I went to a hospital and saw instruments that I had made and knew that they were being used every day to make life better, this gave me great happiness. The same is true of every job you do. Are you a teacher? You enrich the lives of young people every day! Are you a chef? Each meal you cook brings great pleasure into the world! Perhaps you do not love your job, or you work with difficult people. You are still doing important things, contributing your own small piece to the world we live in. We must never forget this. Your efforts today will affect people you will never know. It is your choice whether that effect is positive or negative. You can choose every day, every minute, to act in a way that may uplift a stranger, or else drag them down. The choice is easy. And it is yours to make.

CHAPTER FOURTEEN

Shared sorrow is half sorrow;
shared pleasure is double pleasure.

W E HAD A WONDERFUL LIFE IN AUSTRALIA. After what I had experienced during the war, it truly felt like heaven. My children grew up, had children of their own. I was very happy, but deep down, I had a sadness. My father was fifty-two when he died. My children are older now than when he died. Why? What was all the suffering for?

We suffered and died, and why? For what? For a madman; for no reason. Those six million Jews who died, all the countless more who the Nazis murdered, among them were artists, architects, doctors, lawyers, scientists. It makes me very sad to think of what all those educated, professional men and women might have achieved if they had been able to live. I believe we would have cured cancer by now. But to the Nazis, we were not human. They could not see the waste that murdering us would cause for the world.

For decades, I didn't talk about my experiences in the Holocaust at all. I had no urge to speak about it because I was hurting, and when you are hurt, you want to get away from it, not turn to face how you are feeling. When you lose your mother and father, all your aunties and cousins, almost everyone you have ever loved, how can you speak about it? It was just too painful for me to even think about, all I had been through, all we had lost. And perhaps I wanted to protect my children from it – it would only hurt them to know the truth of things. So I kept my mouth shut.

After many years, though, I began to ask myself another question: why am I alive and not all the others who died so terribly? At first, I decided that God, or whatever higher power, had chosen the wrong people, that I should have died too. But then I began to think that perhaps I was still alive because I had a responsibility to speak about it, and that I had a duty to help to educate the world about the dangers of hate.

My wife is very interested in poetry. I always thought she might have married a poet instead of me, and I just got lucky. Working with words was never my calling. Machines are what I understand – mathematics, science, making things with my hands. But the urge to tell my story became stronger and stronger.

The first time I spoke publicly was to a Catholic church. Close friends of ours in Brighton-Le-Sands were devout

Catholics, and they would invite me to church functions to share my story. This was hard, but it helped me to come out of my shell a little.

In 1972, a group of twenty survivors came together, and said, 'We have to start talking about what happened to us.' The world needed to know. We resolved to make an association, and that if we could raise enough money, we would create a place where we could meet and speak. In 1982, we formalised our group as the Australian Association of Jewish Holocaust Survivors. Years later, as our children became involved, we became the Australian Association of Jewish Holocaust Survivors and Descendants. Then we began to look for a place to found the Sydney Jewish Museum.

One of the members of our association was friends with John Saunders, a very successful businessman who had co-founded the Westfield Group with Frank Lowy. This was at the height of the Westfield Group's growing success, when they were building Westfield Towers in William Street. Mr Saunders put six million dollars into establishing the museum in the Maccabean Hall in Darlinghurst, which was created in 1923 to commemorate the Jewish soldiers who were in the First World War. The Sydney Jewish Museum was born.

In 2007, we expanded the scope of the museum. It now displays not just the history of the Holocaust, but Jewish culture and history in Australia, which goes all the way back to the First Fleet, on which there were sixteen Jews.

In 2011, we established a smaller group where survivors could meet and share their experiences. This was separate to the association, which was open for all Jews dedicated to remembrance of the Holocaust. Ours was just for survivors. We called ourselves Focus, and we were for people who had been through the experience of the concentration camps, who knew what it was to face death every day, to smell the crematorium on the wind as your friends were murdered all around. Those who asked, 'Where shall I go to be safe?' and found there was nowhere to go – who were betrayed, tormented and starved nearly to death.

We formed this group because of the feeling of liberation it gave us to finally tell our stories. I cannot describe how it feels to be in the company of a person who was there, who can feel what you feel the same way, who knows deep down why you react to things the way you do. Other people may try, and that is admirable, but they will never really understand because they have not had this experience. It doesn't matter how many books they read or how hard they try, it is something only we can understand, those who survived the Holocaust.

I lived in a free country and that country became my prison. I have to share this with people who have suffered the same way. There is a saying: shared sorrow is half sorrow; shared pleasure is double pleasure. There is a poem in my mother tongue that expresses our feelings:

Menschen sterben	*(people die)*
Blumen welken	*(flowers wilt)*
Eisen und stahl bricht	*(iron and steel break)*
Aber unsere frundshaft nicht	*(but not our friendship)*

There are survivors who will tell you that this world is bad, that all people have evil inside them, who take no joy from life. These people have not been liberated. Their broken bodies may have walked from the camps 75 years ago, but their broken hearts stayed there. I know survivors who have never been fortunate enough to feel the freedom that comes from putting the burden of suffering down in order to be able to bear up their happiness. Even for me, it took many years to realise that as long as I still held fear and pain in my heart, I would not truly be free.

I do not ask my fellow survivors to forgive the German people. I could not do this myself. But I have been lucky enough and had enough love and friendship in my life that I have been able to release the anger I felt towards them. It does no good to hold onto anger. Anger leads to fear, which leads to hate, which leads to death.

Many from my generation raised their children with the shadow of this hatred and fear. It does your children no good to teach them to be afraid. This is their life! They should celebrate every minute of it. You brought them into this world, you must support them, help them, not push them down with negative thinking. This is an important lesson that we survivors must understand. If you are not free in your heart, don't take away your children's freedom. I always tell my children, 'I brought you into this world because I wanted to love you. You owe me nothing but that. All I need from you is your affection and respect.' This is what I'm proud of – my family is my achievement.

There is nothing so wonderful as to see your family grow and thrive, and to experience the happiness your children feel as they become parents themselves. This is a special bond – when I became a grandfather, I understood, truly, the most important things. I saw the joy that it gave my son to hold his son, and to watch him grow up, and become a child, then a man, to have an education, to fall in love, to build a life – the same joy it gave me to watch my own children. I always tell them they owe me nothing, but do they listen? No! They disobey me and give me everything I could ever ask for.

Every day, I sit down at my table for my coffee, and I am surrounded by pictures of my beautiful children Michael and Andre, their wives Linda and Eva, my grandchildren Danielle, Marc, Phillip and Carly, and my great-grandchildren Lara, Joel, Zoe, Samuel and Toby.

And in them, I see myself, and my beloved Flore. And also my father, and my mother – I see the love that they gave me during their short time on Earth. And that, that is wonderful beyond words. The children will go on, and have their own struggles, and their own triumphs, and will grow, and build, and give back to this society that has given us so much. This is why we live. This is why we work, and strive to pass on the best in us to the next generation.

Kindness is the greatest wealth of all. Small acts of kindness last longer than a lifetime. This lesson, that kindness and generosity and faith in your fellow man are more important than money, is the first and greatest lesson my father ever taught me. And in this way he will always be with us, and always live forever.

Here are the lines I try to live by, and which I like to include when I speak publicly:

May you always have lots of love to share,

Lots of good health to spare,

And lots of good friends who care.

CHAPTER FIFTEEN

What I have to share is not my pain.
What I share is my hope.

FOR A LONG TIME, I DIDN'T WANT TO BURDEN MY children with my story. The first time they ever knew what happened to me was when they heard my story without my knowledge. When my son Michael was already grown, he heard I was to speak at the Great Synagogue about my experiences in the Holocaust, things I had never spoken to him about. He arrived before me and hid behind the heavy curtains so that I would not know he was in attendance. Afterwards, he emerged from behind the curtains in tears to embrace me. This was the first time he ever knew. Since then, my children have been in audiences I have spoken to, but I have never been able to speak to them face-to-face about it. When I try to talk to my son, I see my father in his face. It is just too hard.

Sometimes I think that those of us who didn't tell our stories for so long made a mistake. It seems that sometimes we missed out on a generation who could have helped to make this world a better place, who could have prevented the hatred that is now on the rise everywhere in the world. Perhaps we didn't talk about it enough. There are now deniers of the Holocaust, people who don't believe that it ever happened. Can you imagine? Where do they think six million of us went? Where do they think I got this tattoo?

I feel it is my duty today to tell my story. I know if my mother were here, she would say, 'Do it for me. Try to make this world a better place.'

Over the years, I have seen my message start to spread. It is wonderful. I have spoken to thousands and thousands of schoolchildren, to politicians and professionals. My story is for everyone. And for the past twenty years, I have travelled annually to the Australian Defence Force Academy to speak to the young soldiers. These are the ones I want to reach – the officers, yes, but especially the young men who will be in combat one day. My message is most important to anyone who may hold a gun.

Each time I speak at a school, I say, 'Please put up your hands, anyone who said, "Mum, I love you," when you left the house this morning.' One evening, I returned home and my wife said, 'Eddie, a Mrs Leigh rang. She wants you to call her.'

I rang her back and said, 'Mrs Leigh, you wanted to speak to me?'

'Yes, Mr Jaku. What have you done to my daughter?!'

'Mrs Leigh,' I said, 'I didn't do anything!'

'On the contrary! You made a miracle. She came home and she put her arms around me and whispered in my ear, "Mum, I love you." She's 17 years old! Normally, all she does is argue with me.'

I try to teach this to every young person I meet. Your mother does everything for you. Let her know you appreciate her, let her know that you love her. Why argue with the people you love? Go out on the street, stop a person littering and argue with them. There are a million better people to argue with than your mum!

Every week, I would wake, kiss my wife, put on my suit, and go to the Jewish Museum to tell my story. At first it was the Jewish children who would come to listen. Then the children from other schools across Sydney. Then Australia. And then the adults – the teachers, their friends, their loved ones – began to come to hear what I had to say. This was very touching to me. I began to travel, near and far, as schools and community groups, companies, all sorts of people, young and old, began to contact me, asking me to share the lessons of the Holocaust.

One day, I received a letter from the Government of

Australia. They told me that I had been nominated by a prominent doctor for an Order of Australia medal, and a panel was considering the honour.

On 2 May 2013, I travelled with Flore and my family to Government House in Sydney, where at a ceremony presided over by the Governor of New South Wales, Marie Bashir, I was awarded the Order of Australia Medal for services to the Jewish Community.

What an honour! What a wonderful thing. Once, I was a stateless refugee, knowing nothing but sorrow. Now I am Eddie Jaku, OAM!

Then, in 2019, I was approached by TEDx, an organisation that facilitates talks and speeches from all kinds of people, all over the world, united by the common ideal of 'ideas worth spreading'. They wanted to help me to spread my message to the widest possible audience, over 5000 people in a hall, and hundreds of thousands more who would watch online. On 24 May 2019, I took to the podium for perhaps the biggest speech of my life. I had never spoken to thousands and thousands of people at a time before! After I finished, the whole audience leapt to their feet and would not stop applauding. Afterwards, there were hundreds of people lining up in the hall just to shake my hand or hug me.

In the time since that talk has been put online, more than a quarter of a million people have watched it. The technology is amazing. When I was a child, we were still sending messages by telegram and carrier pigeon! And now I receive mail from people all over the world who have heard my story and been inspired to reach out and tell me how it has moved them. The other day, I received a handwritten letter from a woman in America, a total stranger, who wrote, 'In seventeen minutes you have given me so much to think about, it has changed my whole life.'

Can you imagine? Not that long ago I was reluctant to share my pain with anyone. But this was before I realised that what I have to share is not my pain. What I share is my hope.

In 2020, I was a nominee for 2020 NSW Senior Australian Citizen of the Year. I did not win, but I was in the final four, which is not too bad for a centenarian!

I will keep telling my story for as long as I can. The Jewish Museum will have to kick me out before I retire! When I get tired, I think of all those who did not survive to tell their story. And all those who are too badly hurt after all this time to tell their story. It is for them I speak. And for my parents.

It is hard to tell my story. Sometimes it is very painful. But I ask myself, what will happen when we are all gone? What will happen when all of us survivors have passed away? Will our story fade out of history? Or will we be remembered? It is time for the new generation, the young people, the ones with burning desire to make the world better. They will hear of our pain and inherit our hope.

A field is empty, but if you put in the effort to grow something then you will have a garden. And that's life. Give something, something will come back. Give nothing, nothing will come back. To grow a flower is a miracle: it means you can grow more. Remember that a flower is not just a flower, it is the start of a whole garden.

So I go on telling my story to anyone who wants to know about the Holocaust. If I get through to even one person, it is worth it. And I hope that is you, my new friend. I hope this story goes with you.

EPILOGUE

S EVENTY-FIVE YEARS AGO, IN THE DAYS AFTER the war, I learned of a Nazi being held prisoner in Belgium for his war crimes, and I arranged to see him. I asked him, 'Why? Why would you do this?'

He couldn't answer. He started shaking and crying. He was less than a man, just a shadow of one. I almost felt sorry for him. He did not look evil. He looked pathetic, like he was already dead. And my question remained unanswered.

The older I get, the more I think, why? I cannot help but think about it as if it were an engineering problem I could solve. If I have a machine, I can examine it, diagnose the problem, find out what went wrong, and fix it.

The only answer I can find is hate. Hate is the beginning of a disease, like cancer. It may kill your enemy, but it will destroy you in the process too.

Don't blame others for your misfortunes. No one has ever said that life is easy, but it is easier if you love it. If you hate your life, it becomes impossible to live. This is why I try to be kind. Even though I have suffered, I want to prove to the Nazis that they were wrong. I want to show the people who hate that they are wrong.

So I hate no one, not even Hitler. I do not forgive him. If I forgive, I am a traitor to the six million who died. There is no forgiveness. When I say this, I speak for the six million who cannot speak for themselves. But I also live for them, and live the best life I can.

I promised when I came out of the darkest hours of my life that I would be happy for the rest of my life and smile, because if you smile, the world smiles with you. Life is not always happiness. Sometimes, there are many hard days. But you must remember that you are lucky to be alive – we are all lucky in this way. Every breath is a gift. Life is beautiful if you let it be. Happiness is in your hands.

Seventy-five years ago, I never thought that I would have children, grandchildren and great-grandchildren. I was at the bottom of humanity. And now, here I am.

So, after you put this book down, please, remember to take time to appreciate every moment of your life – the good, the bad. Sometimes there will be tears. Sometimes there will be laughter. And if you are lucky, there will be friends to share it all with, as I have known throughout my life.

Please, every day, remember to be happy, and to make others happy too. Make yourself a friend to the world.

Do this for your new friend, Eddie.

ACKNOWLEDGEMENTS

I NEVER INTENDED WRITING A BOOK AND NEVER thought I would despite having been encouraged to do so by many people over many years, and despite so many of my fellow Holocaust survivors and friends having put their experiences in writing before me.

It was only the approach by Pan Macmillan which finally convinced me to commit my experiences and thoughts to writing at the ripe old age of one hundred years. For that I must sincerely thank publisher Cate Blake and writer Liam Pieper, Cate for her confidence in the project and her persistence, and Liam for his sensitivity and skill in putting my words on the page.

No less important to the endeavour was the encouragement and input of my dear family, my darling wife Flore and my sons Michael and Andre.

This book is for them, and for my grandchildren,

Danielle Jaku-Greenfield, Marc Jaku, Phillip Jaku and Carly Jaku; and my great-grandchildren, Lara, Joel and Zoe Greenfield, and Samuel and Toby Jaku. And for my family near and far: the descendants of my sister Johanna, Leah Wolf and Miriam Oppenheim, my uncle Moritz Eisen (brother of my dear mother) and my aunt Sala Dessauer (sister of my father), both having left Europe for Palestine before the catastrophe. It is also in memory of all my relatives who were murdered by the cruellest society in the history of mankind.

For the six million innocent Jews who cannot speak for themselves, and to the memories of culture, music, and the great potential which perished along with them.

For all the friends I have made in the seventy-five years since the Holocaust.

I must acknowledge and thank the Sydney Jewish Museum and its wonderful staff who have always encouraged me to tell my story to young and old since the museum's opening in 1992. The museum has been a second home to me, and its staff and volunteers a second family.

English is not my first language and with the limitations of advanced age this was not an easy task to undertake. Nevertheless, I hope that readers will find that the effort was worthwhile.

Alone we are powerless, but together we are strong.

I want the world to be a better place and hope humanity might be restored a little by reading this book. I also want to say to you to never give up hope. It is never too late to be kind, polite, and a loving human being.

I wish everybody:

Best of luck

Alles gute

Bonne chance

Your friend,

Eddie Jaku